# SUMMARY GUIDES

# VCE ENGLISH

## UNITS 3 & 4 ASSESSMENT

Melanie Napthine
with Michael E Daniel

First published in 2025 by Insight Publications

Insight Publications Pty Ltd
3/350 Charman Road
Cheltenham VIC 3192
Australia

Tel: +61 3 8571 4950
Email: books@insightpublications.com.au

**www.insightpublications.com.au**



*Summary Guides – VCE English Units 3 & 4 Assessment* / Melanie Napthine with Michael E Daniel

Melanie Napthine asserts the moral right to be identified as the author of this work.

ISBN: 9781923016583 (print)



Publisher: Melanie Napthine
Copy editor: Penny Mansley
Proofreader: Naomi Saligari
Cover and text designer: Melisa Paredes
Printed by Markono Print Media Pte Ltd

Insight Publications is grateful to Clare Heaney and *The Sydney Morning Herald* for permission to reproduce the extract from 'Dear fellow pedestrians, keep to the left, you drongos'.

Insight Publications acknowledges the Traditional Custodians of the Country on which we meet and work, the Boonwurrung People of the Kulin Nation. We pay our respects to their Elders past and present, and extend that respect to all Aboriginal and Torres Strait Islander peoples.

# Contents

# Introduction and assessment overview

This Summary Guide presents guidelines, tips and assessor advice for completing each School-assessed Coursework (SAC) and examination task to help you to maximise your performance in your final year of secondary English study. The tables below summarise the assessment requirements for Units 3 & 4 English.

## Unit 3

| Outcomes | Marks allocated | Assessment tasks |
|---|---|---|
| **Outcome 1** | | |
| Analyse ideas, concerns and values presented in a text, informed by the vocabulary, text structures and language features and how they make meaning. | 40 | An analytical response to text in written form. |
| **Outcome 2** | | |
| Demonstrate effective writing skills by producing their own texts, designed to respond to a specific context and audience to achieve a stated purpose; and explain their decisions made through writing processes. | 40 | Written text constructed in consideration of audience, purpose and context. |
| | 20 | Commentary reflecting on writing processes in relation to the written text. |
| **Total marks** | **100** | |

## Unit 4

| Outcomes | Marks allocated | Assessment tasks |
|---|---|---|
| **Outcome 1** | | |
| Analyse explicit and implicit ideas, concerns and values presented in a text, informed by vocabulary, text structures and language features and how they make meaning. | 40 | An analytical response to text in written form. |
| **Outcome 2** | | |
| Analyse the use of argument and language in persuasive texts, including written text (print or digital) and text in another mode (visual, audio and/or audio visual); and develop and present a point of view text. | 40 | An analytical response to argument and language in one persuasive written text, which must include a different mode (visual or audio or audio visual).<br>The issue for the selected text must have appeared in the media since 1 September of the previous year. |
| | 20 | A point of view oral presentation. |
| **Total marks** | **100** | |

Chapter 01

UNIT 3 AND UNIT 4 OUTCOME 1:

# Analytical text responses

For both Unit 3 Outcome 1 and Unit 4 Outcome 1, you must write an analytical response to a text.

Each outcome is worth 40 marks. The written responses should each be 700 to 900 words.

You have to demonstrate similar knowledge and skills for each outcome; however, your response for the Unit 4 outcome needs to show greater analytical sophistication, due to the skills honed during your senior years of English study. This is reflected in the variations between the descriptions of the outcomes, highlighted below.

## UNIT 3 OUTCOME 1

Analyse ideas, concerns and values presented in a text, informed by the vocabulary, text structures and language features and how they make meaning.

## UNIT 4 OUTCOME 1

Analyse explicit and implicit ideas, concerns and values presented in a text, informed by vocabulary, text structures and language features and how they make meaning.

Your text response should demonstrate close knowledge of a text and analytical skills. It is a formal piece of writing that should present a clear, logically developed interpretation. Your school will probably set this task to be completed in conditions like those of an exam, and you will respond to a previously unseen topic (or possibly a choice of topics).

Text response essays should:

- **respond to the topic**
- **interpret the text**
- **develop the interpretation** in each paragraph
- **draw on evidence** from the text and explain how the evidence reveals aspects of the text's 'big ideas'.

# What you need to know

This section summarises everything you need to know to successfully complete this SAC task.

## Performance descriptors

Your analysis will be assessed against a set of performance descriptors. The 'very high' performance descriptors – which describe a response likely to receive between 33 and 40 marks out of a maximum of 40 – are reproduced in the two left-hand columns in the following table. The right-hand column presents advice on how to achieve this.

<table>
<tr><th colspan="2">'Very high' performance descriptors</th><th rowspan="2">What you need to do</th></tr>
<tr><th>Unit 3 Outcome 1</th><th>Unit 4 Outcome 1</th></tr>
<tr><td rowspan="4">Examines critically the ideas, concerns and values, including discussion of character, setting and other aspects of the text.</td><td rowspan="4">Examines critically ideas, concerns and values presented in the text, including discussion of character, setting and other aspects of the text.</td><td>Draw examples from throughout the text, referring to a range of characters, situations and events.</td></tr>
<tr><td>Refer to settings and contexts and explain how these impact characters' attitudes and choices.</td></tr>
<tr><td>Discuss values that are stated explicitly by the narrator or characters, as well as those implied by characters' decisions and the consequences of their actions.</td></tr>
<tr><td>Think about where and when the author was writing (their context), who they were writing for (their audience) and what they might have wanted the audience to think and/or feel.</td></tr>
<tr><td rowspan="3">Examines critically relevant text structures, language features and vocabulary choices that convey complex and nuanced ideas.</td><td rowspan="3">Examines critically relevant text structures, language features and vocabulary choices to convey relevant, nuanced and complex ideas.</td><td>Present a view of the text's overall meaning.</td></tr>
<tr><td>Justify your view with close discussion of features (e.g. characterisation, setting, structure, language).</td></tr>
<tr><td>Support your statements about the text's meaning with specific textual evidence, including quotations.</td></tr>
</table>

 

| 'Very high' performance descriptors | | What you need to do |
|---|---|---|
| **Unit 3 Outcome 1** | **Unit 4 Outcome 1** | |
| Examines critically and clarifies the connections between the ideas and values of the text in response to a topic. | Examines critically and clarifies the connections between the ideas and values of the text in a critical consideration of the topic and its implications. | Develop a logical argument about the text's meaning and in response to the essay topic. |
| | | Create a clear beginning (introduction), middle (body paragraphs) and end (conclusion). |
| Integrates relevant textual evidence with precision and control to examine critically the ways in which ideas are presented in the text in consideration of the topic. | Integrates relevant textual evidence with precision and control to examine the ways ideas are presented in the text. | Select evidence carefully, drawing on a range of aspects of the text (e.g. characters, structure). |
| | | When citing evidence from the text, always connect it to what the author is aiming to communicate about an idea or value. |
| | | Maintain a focus on the topic, including its subtleties (e.g. multiple key words or limiting words). |
| Composes a complex exposition with sequenced, coherent and cohesive paragraphs.<br>Uses nuanced and appropriate language and accurate metalanguage to examine the text fluently and critically. | Composes a complex exposition with sequenced, coherent and cohesive paragraphs.<br>Uses nuanced and appropriate language and accurate metalanguage to examine the text fluently and critically. | Communicate your thinking about the text and your response to the topic. |
| | | Structure your essay clearly, with well-written, logically connected introductory, body and concluding paragraphs. |
| | | Link words, ideas and paragraphs fluently. |
| | | Use language clearly and precisely. |
| | | Spell and punctuate correctly. |
| | | Use correct syntax (the order of words in a sentence) and varied sentence structures. |
| | | Do not use informal language features (e.g. contractions, colloquial expressions). |
| | | Use appropriate metalanguage for analysing textual features. |

## Key knowledge and skills

Knowing your text well is vital to achieving good results in the SAC tasks and the exam. This section gives an overview of the key aspects of your text that you should be prepared to analyse. Remember: there is no 'correct' reading of any text. Assessors will not penalise you if your interpretation differs from theirs, as long as you present a well-reasoned argument supported by strong textual evidence.

**Use the tables in this section as templates to make notes in your workbook or on your computer.**

### Characters

Characters are one of the primary vehicles through which text creators explore ideas and values. Aspects of characters that are useful for this include their personality, situation, relationships and development as a result of events in the plot.

| Characters | |
|---|---|
| Is a particular character the 'moral compass' (embodies values the author endorses)? What are these values? | |
| Is a particular character the villain (embodies values the author condemns)? What are these values? | |
| What strengths and weaknesses does each character possess? | |
| How do the characters fit in or respond to their setting? | |
| Which characters reflect or are typical of their society? Which characters challenge or reject the values of their society? | |
| How and why do the characters develop and change? What situations, events or relationships force them to make important choices? | |
| What do the characters and their development reveal about important ideas in the text? What bigger messages are being communicated? What values are endorsed or criticised? | |

 

## Plot

It is the plot that initially engages the audience. For example, the reader of Charlotte Brontë's *Jane Eyre* wonders whether Jane and Rochester will be reunited. Events in the plot facilitate characterisation (by showing how characters react to situations) and support the author's messages about key ideas and values.

The *climax* is the high point of the plot, which foreshadows the ending. It can be a good place to examine what the text is communicating about its main ideas.

| Plot | |
|---|---|
| How does the text begin? What is at stake for the characters? | |
| Identify a significant turning point. Why is it important? What changes for the main character/s? | |
| Are there flashbacks or flashforwards? What is their effect? | |
| When is the climax? What happens? | |
| What happens in the end? Do the main characters find happiness and/or justice? Why / why not? | |
| Are any questions left unresolved? Why might this be? | |

## Setting

The setting (time and place) of a text shapes the ideas it explores and the values it critiques or supports. The setting can also illuminate aspects of character. For example, consider Miles Franklin's novel *My Brilliant Career*. The setting – rural Australia in the 1890s – creates the conditions for the ambitious Sybylla Melvyn to challenge the social constraints placed on women in that time and place.

| Setting | |
|---|---|
| When and where does the story take place? | |
| How does the setting affect the characters and their situations and choices? | |
| What is the significance of the setting? (Consider whether the same events could occur in different places and times and still unfold in the same way.) What does the setting reveal about key concerns of the text? | |

## Narrative point of view

Your text might be written in the third or the first person (or, rarely, the second person). The choice of narrative point of view affects the reader's interpretation. If it is written in the first person (that is, if the story is told from the perspective of the narrator), the reader might be encouraged to share this character's thoughts and feelings. If it is written in the third person, the focus might be on the perspective of a certain character, encouraging the reader to empathise with this viewpoint. An omniscient third-person narrator, on the other hand, can suggest objectivity and reliability.

| Narrative point of view | |
|---|---|
| How is the story told: in the first person or the third person? Does the text show one or multiple perspectives? | |
| Why has the author chosen this viewpoint? What does it allow them to explore or express that a different viewpoint might not? | |

Consider also the tense used. In some texts, the present tense is used extensively to give the story a sense of dynamism and realism. Past tense, by contrast, can suggest completion and distance from events.

## Structure

The structuring decisions made by a text creator help them to convey particular messages and create specific effects. For example, a text might be divided into chapters, sections, or acts and scenes. Where the creator chooses to position these breaks is important for creating suspense, drawing attention to ideas or points of tension, raising questions in the audience's mind and communicating ideas and values.

 

Similar effects can be created by varying the sequence of events. Plots can be linear/chronological (where events are told in the order in which they occur), fragmented (where flashbacks and flashforwards are used to relay events in a non-chronological order) or circular (where the narrative begins and ends in the same setting). Another structural variation is where one story takes place within another story (called an embedded narrative).

| Structure | |
|---|---|
| Is the text a novel, play, film, short story or poetry collection, or nonfiction work? How does the form impact the way in which the story is told? | |
| How is the narrative arranged? For example, is it divided into chapters or acts? Does the text use flashbacks or flashforwards? Is the plot linear, circular or fragmented? | |

## Language

Language is, of course, the main vehicle used by a text creator to communicate. Consider the language style and how it supports the writer's ideas or messages. The language in Yōko Ogawa's novel *The Memory Police*, for instance, is mostly simple and spare, reflecting the narrator's moral purity.

Symbolism is an element of language (or of visual language in a film or play). For example, in Billy Wilder's film *Sunset Boulevard*, Norma's dark house symbolises her delusion, while the sunglasses she wears on her outing to the studio indicate her difficulty facing the light, which symbolises the truth.

| Language | |
|---|---|
| Are there recurring images and symbols in the text? What are they, and what is their significance? | |
| What are the significant features of the text's language? Does it tend to be sparse or highly language? Does it tend to be sparse or highly descriptive? How does this support the way important ideas are communicated? | |

## Ideas and values

Texts explore ideas and promote and/or challenge specific values. For example, *My Brilliant Career* explores how colonial Australian society limited women's choices, and *Sunset Boulevard* is critical of many aspects of the movie industry.

To identify the main *ideas* in a text, look for repeated words or topics of conversation among the characters. For instance, in Pat Barker's novel *Regeneration*, the words 'war', 'memory', 'remember' and 'trauma' appear frequently, indicating that these are important concerns of the text.

Also consider what matters most to the main character/s. What do they want? What do they struggle with? What do they learn? Try brainstorming key words that come to mind when you think about the text. These should point you to its most important ideas.

To determine the *values* endorsed or condemned in a text, think about which characters are rewarded and which are punished. If someone is rewarded for an action, the writer might be indicating that the action is good and that their society is fair and just. However, if someone is punished for doing the right thing, their action might be admirable but their society unjust. Similarly, if someone does the wrong thing and suffers for it, this suggests the society in which they live is mostly fair. However, if someone benefits from doing the wrong thing, the author might be criticising not only the behaviour but also the society that accepts or ignores it.

Another way to identify the values in a text is to list the characters and their actions according to whether they are portrayed as 'good' or 'evil'. Ask yourself why the author has led readers to regard the characters and their actions in this way.

| Ideas and values | |
|---|---|
| What ideas are explored in the text? What issues and dilemmas must the characters face? | |
| What values and attitudes are endorsed or critiqued in the text? How is this achieved? | |
| What is the text trying to tell us about life? | |

## Special features of different text types

Different text types employ special features to create meaning. For example, costuming in films is very important, conveying information about the setting as well as the personalities and circumstances of the characters. In a play script, stage directions guide the reader's interpretation of characters and events. In poetry, stanzas and line breaks contribute to rhythm and connect ideas.

| Special features of different text types | |
|---|---|
| What features are associated with the text's form? | |
| How does the author use each feature to communicate their ideas? | |

# What you need to do

This section summarises everything you need to do to complete these SAC tasks.

## Prepare for the SAC tasks

In addition to the work you do in class for Unit 3 Outcome 1 and Unit 4 Outcome 1, you can prepare by following the suggestions below.

### Read

- **Read or watch your text** several times. The first reading should be done during the December–January holidays. Subsequent readings can be done when you study the text as a class.
- **Read study guides** on your text. But remember that these are aids only, *not* substitutes for your own careful reading and analysis of your text.
- **Research** the context in which your text was written and (if this is different) in which it is set.
- **Memorise the spellings** of important place names, characters' names and other significant vocabulary associated with your text. Try writing the words on sticky notes and placing them on your computer or the wall near your desk, so that you see them regularly. You could also create a screensaver or phone background using the words.

### Write

- **Make notes on and annotate your text**, highlighting key quotations and aspects of big-idea development through plot points, characters, setting, narrative structure and other textual features.
- **Create a bank of quotations** covering different aspects of the text, including ideas and values. Choose quotations you could use when discussing various aspects of a text, including characters, ideas and structural elements.

- **Create a list of structural features** and their effects.
- **Use a thesaurus** to create a bank of synonyms for significant words and concepts associated with your text.

## Plan your text response

This section presents some guidelines and advice for unpacking a topic, generating ideas, selecting evidence and creating a plan in a limited time.

### Unpacking a topic

You will be given an essay topic, which you will need to analyse closely to develop a well-structured, relevant response. Begin by unpacking the topic to clarify what you are being asked to do.

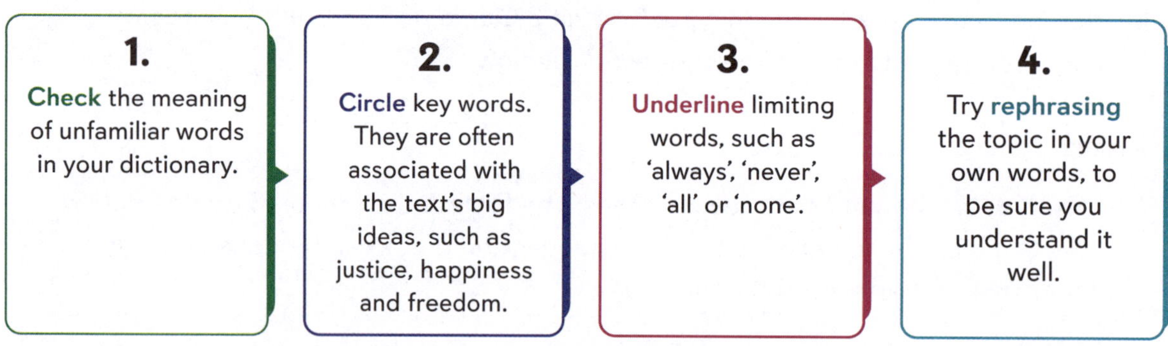


Most topics contain a *proposition* (or concept) that needs to be resolved, then a *direction* or *question* (such as 'Discuss' or 'Do you agree?').

If a topic contains a limiting word (such as 'always', 'all', 'none' or 'never'), only one example from the text is needed to challenge it. The use of a limiting word in an essay topic usually suggests that the proposition *should* be challenged.

However, some topics contain a proposition that is *not* meant to be challenged. Instead, you need to consider how the text explores the idea/s in the proposition.

Certain topics require you to define or explain the meanings of key words and phrases – particularly when their meaning is open to different interpretations. For example, consider the following topic.

> In *Twelfth Night*, Shakespeare suggests that the end justifies the means. To what extent do you agree?

This type of topic gives you what is known as the 'right of reasonable definition', meaning that in your introduction, you should clearly define the key phrase (in this example, 'the end justifies the means'). Your definition must be reasonable and consistent with the ideas and values in the text.

 

WRITE

**The table below summarises some common types of essay topics. In the middle column, there are example topics related to different texts.**

**Identify a second example essay topic for each topic type, using your text. You can source topics from:**

- **practice essays you have written previously**
- **your teacher**
- **study guides**
- **past VCAA exam papers**
- **past practice exam papers.**

| Topic types | Example essay topics | What to do |
|---|---|---|
| 'Discuss' | 1 The female characters in *Ghost Wall* are powerless victims. Discuss.<br>2 | You might consider arguments and evidence both for and against the statement. However, you still need to have a clear contention (a main stance or argument in response to the essay question). |
| 'Do you agree?' and 'To what extent do you agree?' | 1 In *Jane Eyre*, the characters are victims of forces beyond their control. Do you agree?<br>2 | You can agree, disagree or partly agree. Your own point of view must be clear, and you must give evidence from the text to back up your argument. |
| 'To what extent ...?' | 1 To what extent do the protagonists in *Every Move You Make* find a sense of fulfilment?<br>2 | Your response must judge the degree to which the proposition in the question is true. Possible points of view include entirely, mainly, partially, hardly and not at all. (A common mistake is to explore the idea in the topic without communicating a clear interpretation of the degree to which the proposition is true.) |

➪

| Topic types | Example essay topics | What to do |
|---|---|---|
| **Topics that include quotations** | 1 'You do not have to be good.'<br>For Mary Oliver, there are more important qualities than virtue. Discuss.<br>2 | The quotation should direct the focus of your response; you should refer to it in your essay. Identify where it occurs in the text and consider the context. Is it said by a character, or does it come from the narrative voice? How reliable is that voice?<br>Think of other textual evidence that supports the idea in the quotation, as well as any evidence that suggests something different. |
| **Direct questions** | 1 What do the characters in *Orbital* learn about the world through their experiences?<br>2 | Answer the question by considering these prompts:<br>**What?** Give information from the text about the idea in the topic.<br>**How?** Explore how the author communicates the idea. |
| **Topics focused on audience response or interpretation** | 1 In *Sunset Boulevard*, the audience is positioned to have little sympathy for Gillis and Desmond. Discuss.<br>2 | Focus on how the text shapes the audience's responses. What aspects of the text and its construction lead the audience to certain conclusions or interpretations? |

 

| Topic types | Example essay topics | What to do |
|---|---|---|
| **Topics that invite you to compare or contrast** | 1 For the characters in *We Have Always Lived in the Castle*, being true to oneself is more important than being accepted by others. Do you agree?<br>2 | Communicate a clear point of view on the statement or question. Include comparison in each body paragraph, using words and phrases like 'similarly', 'likewise', 'in addition', 'moreover', 'on the other hand', 'however' and 'although'. |
| **Structural or 'how' topics** | 1 How does *We Come with This Place* convey the trauma of experiencing racism?<br>2 | Explore how the author creates meaning through the structural features of the text. Use words and phrases like 'through', 'by', 'the use of' and 'with' to retain focus on what the text's creator is doing and why. |
| **Topics with multiple ideas or parts** | 1 To what extent does *Regeneration* suggest that individuals and society are capable of change?<br>2 | Address all parts of the topic, giving roughly the same amount of attention to each part. Here, you need to discuss both individuals *and* society. |

Even if you are not responding to an explicit 'How' topic, you should always discuss the strategies used by the text creator to communicate the specific ideas you are discussing.

## Generating ideas, selecting evidence and forming a contention

After you have unpacked the essay topic, you need to decide your opinion on the topic so that you can form a contention for your response. Begin by *brainstorming*.

One effective brainstorming method is to write the topic in the centre of a page and jot down ideas around it. Include examples and quotations (evidence) that support the ideas.

Many topics contain a proposition that is meant to be challenged. For this type of topic, a useful brainstorming method is to draw two columns, headed 'For' and 'Against', and note ideas and evidence in the columns that support or contradict the proposition in the topic.

Ask yourself as many questions as you can about the topic – in particular, *why* and *how* questions.

Next, *organise your material*. Identify the best ideas in your brainstorm, for which you have strong textual evidence. Colour-code the material so that it is clear which evidence connects to which ideas.

You will not be writing everything you know about the text. Instead, select *relevant details* to respond to the topic, including the ideas and values embedded in the text, together with textual evidence (e.g. plot points, character choices, structural features and quotations). The better you know your text, the more details you will be able to draw on when selecting evidence for your essay.

Now, *form a contention* by writing down your opinion on the topic in a single sentence. Remember that a strong response acknowledges the complexity of the topic. If there is a statement in the topic, you may disagree with it partly or completely, as long as you can support your view with textual evidence.

 

## Creating a plan

An example of a brief but effective text response plan is shown below.

| | |
|---|---|
| **Introduction** | Your contention<br>Outline of the reasons you will present to support your contention |
| **Body paragraph 1** | Your most important reason<br>Evidence 1<br>Evidence 2<br>Evidence 3 |
| **Body paragraph 2** | Your second most important reason<br>Evidence 1<br>Evidence 2<br>Evidence 3 |
| **Body paragraph 3** | Your third most important reason<br>Evidence 1<br>Evidence 2<br>Evidence 3 |
| **Body paragraph 4** | Your fourth most important reason and/or consideration of alternative interpretations<br>Evidence 1<br>Evidence 2<br>Evidence 3 |
| **Conclusion** | Summary of your argument, linking it to the text's big ideas |

The importance of planning the structure and organisation of your text response is illustrated in the tree diagram on the next page. This tree provides a useful visual analogy of an effective text response. If you don't support your analysis with evidence, your piece of writing is like a tree without leaves. However, if you *only* list evidence, without linking it to the ideas in the topic and text, your writing is like a pile of leaves (without any structure, form or organisation).

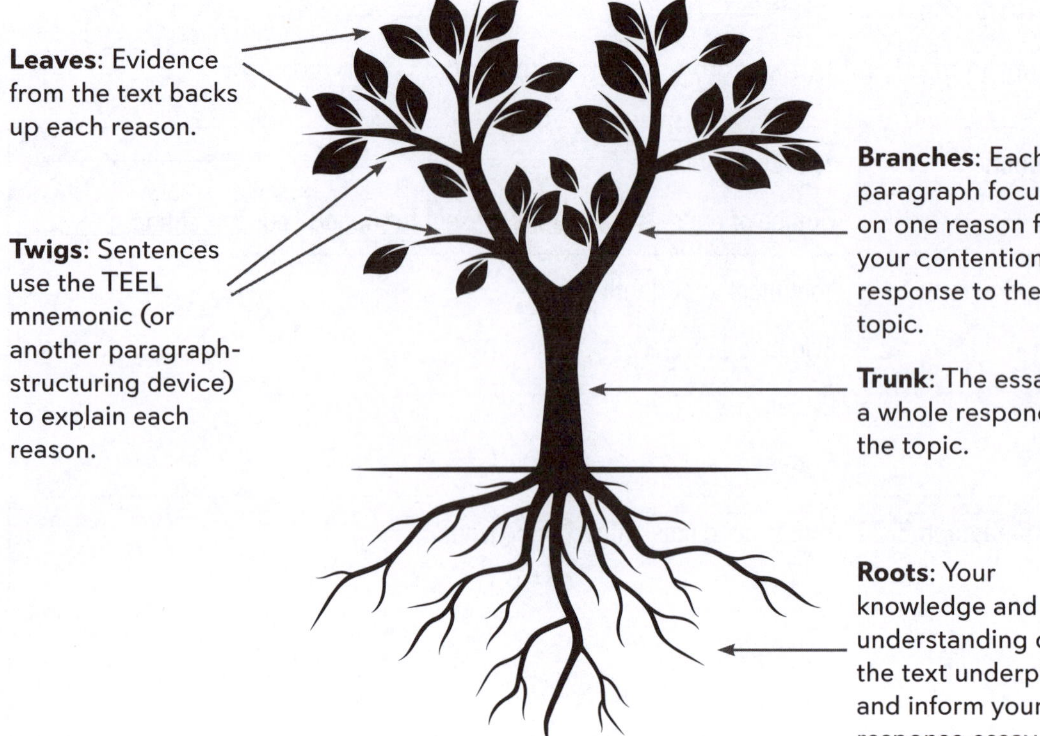


WRITE

**For each essay topic you added to the table on pages 11–13, complete the following tasks.**

- **Create a main contention in response to the topic.**
- **Produce a dot-point plan that includes three or four supporting arguments or reasons for your interpretation, as well as notes about textual evidence to back up each.**

A key element of this task is *relevance*. Make sure you do the following.

› **Answer the question.** Have you addressed exactly what the question is asking you?

› **Answer the whole question.** Have you responded adequately to *all* elements of the question?

› **Answer nothing but the question.** Have you ensured that none of the material in your essay is off topic? Remember, the task does not require you to demonstrate how much you know about the text. Instead you need to show how well you can draw on your textual knowledge and understanding to respond to the particular essay topic.

 

# Writing an analytical text response

This section presents advice for writing a fluent, well-structured analytical text response.

## Elements of analytical text responses

Key elements of text analyses include the following.

### Introduction

You might structure your introductory paragraph like this:

**Sentence 1.** Identify the main textual elements: text title, author, text type and a link to the topic.

**Sentence 2.** State a contention that clearly expresses your response to the topic, using synonyms for key terms in the topic.

**Sentence 3 and subsequent sentences.** List your main points in the order they will be explored in the body paragraphs.

You can use the following sentence starters in introductions.

| Introduction sentence starters |
|---|
| The author/director/playwright/poet considers the idea that … |
| [Title of text] suggests that … |
| [Title of text] explores the ideas of … |
| While [title of text] suggests that …, it also suggests that … |
| The author/director/playwright/poet of [title of text] uses [techniques] to convey the point that … |
| [Title of text] shows the characters to be … Through this, the text creator endorses/condemns … |
| |

In the introduction, keep the emphasis on your main argument; avoid introducing detailed evidence.

WRITE

1 **Add another sentence starter to the blank row of the table above.**

2 **Use one of the sentence starters above to create a sentence about your text.**

## Body paragraphs

The body of the essay should contain at least three paragraphs. Write one paragraph for each of your main points. Your paragraphs could be structured using the mnemonic device TEEL. (You might repeat these steps within a single paragraph.)

**Topic sentence.** State clearly the point being explored in the paragraph, linking it to the key words and ideas in the topic and to your contention.

**Elaboration.** Develop the point, explaining its significance in terms of the topic.

**Evidence.** Support your point with examples and evidence from the text, including at least two quotations.

**Link.** Refer back to the topic and your contention and connect forward to the next paragraph.

In your body paragraphs, try to step back from the specifics of the evidence you include to analyse what the writer reveals through that evidence about human nature or the importance of a topic-related idea (e.g. courage, regret, hope).

You can use the following sentence starters in body paragraphs.

| Body paragraph sentence starters |
|---|
| The author director/playwright/poet shows that … by using techniques such as … |
| [Character's name] is depicted as …, as shown when they …, supporting the author's depiction of their society as … |
| [Character's name] undergoes a significant change in the text. They are … at the beginning of the text but become … because of their experiences, suggesting that [link to idea]. |
| The author/director/playwright/poet's interest in the idea of … is expressed through the experiences of [characters' names], who all … |
| The structure of the text reflects the idea of … |
| [Event/situation in the text] illustrates the author's point of view on [idea]. |
| A recurring symbol in the text is … which is associated with … |
| [Title of text] endorses the values of … |
| [Idea] is evident when [event in the text]. |
| The main characters embody [value]. The author promotes/disapproves of this value, as shown by [event in the text]. |
| |

 

WRITE

1 Add another sentence starter to the blank row of the table on the opposite page.

2 Use one of the sentence starters on the opposite page to create a sentence about your text.

## Linking words

One of the important qualities of a high-level text analysis is *cohesion*. A cohesive text is an integrated piece in which the ideas are connected and the writing flows smoothly.

If a response has been carefully planned, the ideas should follow each other logically. You can also convey a sense of unity by using appropriate linking words and phrases.

The following words and phrases help to connect points fluently.

| Use to discuss a similar idea |
|---|
| Furthermore |
| Similarly |
| Moreover |
| Consequently |
| Therefore |

| Use to present a different idea |
|---|
| However |
| Nevertheless |
| On the other hand |
| By contrast |
| Conversely |

'Also' and 'but' are effective linking words, but they are best used to join phrases together *within* a sentence, not to *start* a sentence.

## Quotations

Quotations from the text are an important form of evidence to support your contention. You should include at least two quotations in every paragraph of your response. The most effective way to do this is to embed quotations within your sentences. The following list gives you some guidelines.

- **The shorter the quotation, the better**, in general. If you can remember only key words, paraphrase the rest and include the key words (inside quote marks) in the paraphrase.

  e.g. Despite their expertise and experiences, the characters in *Orbital* still sometimes struggle to accept that the Earth is not 'the centre of everything'.

- **Use square brackets to modify part of a quotation** so that it fits into your sentence grammatically (e.g. if you need to insert a pronoun or change the tense of a verb).

  e.g. Shaun reflects that the moon landing 'put [him] off' being an astronaut due to his father's and uncle's reactions to it.

  (The original quotation reads 'It put *me* off.')

- **Use an ellipsis in place of deleted words** if you want to shorten a quotation.

  e.g. The astronauts are happy to disregard certain societal rules while on board: 'astronauts and cosmonauts are like cats … can't be herded'.

- **Avoid using the words 'quotation' and 'quote'**, as they can sound awkward. Instead, incorporate the quotation naturally into your sentence.

  e.g. The astronauts come to feel that, overwhelmingly, 'the planet is shaped by … human want'.

- **Avoid beginning a paragraph or sentence with a quotation**. It is better to cite evidence *after* you have developed the point that the evidence supports.

  e.g. The astronauts' sense of perspective is subject to distortion and change because of their experiences, causing them to feel that their actions as humans on Earth are both important and as insignificant as 'windblown leaves'.

WRITE

**Write a sentence about your text that includes a quotation. Use the guidelines listed in this section to incorporate the quotation smoothly into your own writing.**

## References to authorial intent

Authors use texts to explore specific ideas and endorse or critique certain values. In your text response, you need to analyse the ideas and values the author has embedded in the text. This means you should refer to *authorial intent* (what the author is trying to communicate to readers).

This can often be done by framing sentences to focus on what the author is doing. Consider the following examples, which discuss Debra Dank's nonfiction text *We Come with This Place*. The underlined words draw attention to authorial intent.

**Original sentence:** Dank and her family are victims of the widespread and often unacknowledged racism in Australia.

**Improved sentence:** Dank <u>condemns</u> the widespread and often unacknowledged racism in Australian attitudes <u>through</u> her depiction of the treatment that members of her family receive at the hands of 'ordinary' white characters.

 

**Original sentence:** Dank's father exhibits resilience and integrity.

**Improved sentence:** Dank characterises her father as resilient and a man of integrity.

REVISE

**Find a sentence in an essay you have written that could be improved by referring to the author's intentions. Revise the sentence, using the examples above as models.**

## Conclusion

A conclusion draws your discussion to a close. It is usually the last thing the marker of your work will read, so it is worth practising writing conclusions that create an impression of thoughtful reflection.

You might structure your concluding paragraph like this:

**Sentence 1.** Sum up your supporting points and evidence.

**Sentence 2.** Restate your central argument but avoid using the same words as in the introduction.

**Sentences 3 and 4.** Include one or two big-picture statements about the text's significance and wider meaning.

You can use the following sentence starters in conclusions.

| Conclusion sentence starters |
| --- |
| In summary, it is apparent that … |
| The evidence suggests that … |
| In conclusion, it can be seen that … |
| As has been shown, … |
| The text demonstrates … |
| |

WRITE

1 **Add your own sentence starter to the blank row of the table above.**

2 **Use one of the sentence starters above to create a sentence about your text.**

## Improve your text response

You will have the opportunity to write and draft practice essays before your SAC task. It's important to make the most of this process and to act on your teacher's feedback, which will help you to produce a high-level final product.

### Editing your work

You can use a checklist like the one on the next page to edit your work. Complete the checklist after each draft of a practice text analysis. Aim to tick every cell of the final column.

Begin by focusing on the big picture, reading your first draft for *structure* and *meaning*. Then, focus on the small picture, looking for *spelling and grammatical errors* and making sure your *language choices are appropriate*.

| What you should check | First draft | Second draft | Third draft |
|---|---|---|---|
| **Structure and meaning** | | | |
| The introduction includes a clear contention that addresses the topic. | | | |
| The body of the essay presents a clear, consistent line of argument. | | | |
| Each body paragraph contains a clear, relevant topic sentence. | | | |
| There is a link to the topic in each paragraph, and you have used linking words to show a logical development of ideas. | | | |
| The conclusion refers to and is clearly still addressing the topic. | | | |
| **Language** | | | |
| The names of characters and places are correctly spelled. | | | |
| At least two relevant quotations are included in each body paragraph. | | | |
| Sentence structures are varied; you have used some simple and some complex sentences. | | | |
| The present tense is used throughout (except in quotations). | | | |
| Appropriate formal language is used at all times (e.g. no first-person 'I'). | | | |
| Vocabulary is precise and varied. | | | |

 

EDIT

1 Working with an early draft of your essay, identify and correct or rewrite:

- three spelling, punctuation or grammatical errors
- at least three vague or uninteresting words or phrases that could be replaced with more precise or interesting words or phrases
- at least two long and complicated sentences that could be replaced with simpler and clearer sentences.

2 Swap essays with a partner and, after reading each other's essay, complete the following tasks.

- Identify one paragraph that you think works well. Explain why.
- Identify one paragraph that you think could be improved. Give a specific suggestion for improving it.
- Decide what you think is the main contention or argument of the essay. Discuss this with your partner: is it what they intended?

## Common mistakes and tips for top responses

The table below outlines some common mistakes made in text responses and explains how to fix them.

| Common mistakes | Solutions |
|---|---|
| Digressing or veering off topic | Even if you disagree with the statement in the topic, your response must still engage with it. Read your work from the start each time you write a new paragraph. You can check whether you are on track and, if necessary, remove any irrelevancies. |
| Telling the story or describing the text rather than analysing it | Remember: your reader already knows the text well. Keep plot details to a minimum and always explain why you have mentioned them. |
| Not engaging with the ideas and values in the text | Make sure you connect your argument and textual evidence to the big ideas the author is exploring. |
| Repeating the same point or evidence | Your contention should be supported by at least three strong, clearly separate reasons, each backed up by evidence from the text. Check that, together, your reasons build a strong, logical response to the topic. |

| Common mistakes | Solutions |
|---|---|
| Writing poorly | An important performance descriptor relates to the proficient use of the English language. Even in a time-limited situation, allow approximately five minutes to read over your work to check for clunky or unclear expression and spelling and punctuation errors. |

Keep in mind the following advice for producing a high-level text response.

- Follow the **direction words** carefully to write the kind of answer required.
- Take note of any **limiting words** and avoid generalising too much.
- **Keep quotations short and selective**, and learn the spelling of character and place names.
- Refer to the text's **form** (e.g. if you are writing about *Sunset Boulevard*, make some references to film techniques, such as close-ups; if you are writing about *Twelfth Night*, make some references to stage directions).
- Refer to **how the writer or director creates meaning and conveys ideas**. Some topics will take the form of a 'how' question, but even if the topic centres on characters or themes, you should still demonstrate an awareness of the way in which the text is crafted to create particular effects.
- **Use appropriately formal language.** Do not use slang or abbreviations, unless you are quoting someone.
- Present **an original and thoughtful interpretation** to demonstrate engagement with the text. Do not only explore the obvious ideas in the text or use only the most obvious examples as evidence. Instead, show that you know the text well and have thought about it deeply by presenting a nuanced argument supported by a wide range of evidence, including less obvious examples (e.g. quotations from minor characters or events related to subplots).

 

# Chapter 02

## UNIT 3 OUTCOME 2 (TASKS 1 AND 2):

# Original texts and reflective commentaries

Unit 3 Outcome 2 has two tasks: writing original texts and writing reflective commentaries. The tasks are discussed separately in this chapter.

## ORIGINAL TEXTS

For Unit 3 Outcome 2 Task 1, you must produce your own original text/s, which should respond to a specific context, target a particular audience and aim to achieve a purpose.

You might be required to produce one text of 700 to 900 words, which is worth 40 marks. Alternatively, you might be asked to produce two shorter texts of 400 to 450 words, with each worth 20 marks.

## What you need to know

This section summarises everything you need to know to successfully complete this SAC task.

### Performance descriptors

Your writing will be assessed against a set of performance descriptors. The 'very high' performance descriptors – which describe a response likely to receive between 33 and 40 marks out of a maximum of 40 – are reproduced in the left-hand column of the table on the next page. The right-hand column presents advice on how to achieve this.

| 'Very high' performance descriptors | What you need to do |
|---|---|
| Develops a series of ideas that are meaningfully connected. | Ensure your piece explores significant ideas connected to each other, your Framework and to the title and stimulus material you are given. While you don't need to state explicitly the ways in which you are doing this, the connections must be clear to the person marking your work. |
| | Begin your planning by identifying the idea/s you will focus on. |
| Connects audience, purpose and context through the specific use of voice, tone, register and metalanguage. | Before you start writing, establish a clear idea of your specific audience and purpose, and the context in which you will be writing. |
| | Keep your audience, purpose and context uppermost in mind as you write, making careful language choices to cater for these. |
| Engages creatively with text structure, language features and vocabulary that promote the exploration of ideas. | Apply to your writing the strategies and skills you have learned from studying the mentor texts. |
| | Don't be afraid to try new ideas and experiment with form and language, especially in practice pieces, as this will help you to develop your own style. |
| | Remember that your focus needs to be on ideas: your choices about structure and language should be made with this in mind. |
| Creates an apt, sustained and individual voice. | Be yourself! Although you should draw on the effective writing models of the mentor texts, the voice you create should be authentically your own. |
| | Draw on your own ideas, experiences and feelings in your work. |
| | Ensure your voice is appropriate to your audience and purpose. |
| Employs considered and intentional conventions of language to text structure across the whole text. | Be familiar with and make purposeful use of the key features of your chosen text type. |
| | Take time to plan your piece so that its structure is considered and supports your exploration and development of ideas. |
| | Make sure your tone, register and vocabulary choices are appropriate to your text type as well as to your purpose and intended audience. |

 

## Key knowledge and skills

This SAC task is all about the depth of your thinking about the Framework and the quality of your writing. Your study of the Framework should lead you to develop your own ideas connected to it that you can explore in your writing.

You should be familiar with the sorts of writing associated with the four main purposes of writing: *to explain, to reflect, to express* and *to argue*. You should also understand the key features of the text types you might use, as well as aspects of the mentor texts associated with your Framework that you might draw on.

### The Framework

Your writing for this SAC task should show that you have reflected on the main idea in the Framework you are studying. The best way to build on the work you do in class and the group discussions you have about the Framework is to read widely.

Seek out news stories, fictional texts, podcasts and other texts that stimulate your thinking about Framework ideas. Make notes not only about the content and writing strategies of these texts but also about your own responses to others' ideas.

Keep notes that you can add to as you study and read about Framework ideas. You could organise your notes into the following types of information.

| | |
|---|---|
| Your own reflections on key ideas | |
| Reflections on key ideas sourced from other people (e.g. classmates and friends, writers, historical figures) | |
| Your thoughts on texts that expand your thinking about Framework ideas (e.g. books, articles, poems, movies, podcasts, television programs) | |
| Images that inspire reflection on Framework ideas | |
| Quotations connected to Framework ideas | |

**Use the table above as a template to make notes about Framework ideas; write an example of each type of information.**

## Text types

The following table identifies some forms of original texts and their main features. (Note that other forms are possible, including hybrid forms; your teacher will tell you whether other forms are acceptable.)

| Forms | Features |
| --- | --- |
| **Short stories** | Focus on a specific moment or event |
| | Usually told from one point of view |
| | Reveal information slowly to build suspense or tension |
| | Include a hook, exposition, rising tension and resolution |
| | Feature only a few characters, focusing primarily on one |
| | Use symbolism, imagery and figurative language, as well as vivid descriptions based on sensory detail |
| **Diary entries**<br>**Personal reflections** | Reflect personal thoughts in first-person voice |
| | Include reflection on big ideas, rather than simply recounting events |
| **Letters** | Include address, date and formal greeting |
| | May express personal thoughts and feelings, as well as reflections on ideas |
| | May use sentence fragments and unconventional sentence structures and punctuation to reflect characterisation |
| **Memoirs**<br>**Autobiography extracts**<br>**Biography extracts** | Assumed to be truthful |
| | Written in the first person (autobiographies and memoirs) |
| | Written in the third person (biographies) |
| | Usually use formal or standard register, depending on the purpose and audience |
| | Create a personal tone |
| | Often include anecdotes and facts |

 

| Forms | Features |
|---|---|
| **Speeches**<br>**Monologues** | Use the first-person voice |
| | Language reflects character's or persona's personality |
| | Often positioned in a larger text at a moment of indecision or crisis |
| | Often use an engaging opening to capture attention and a powerful, memorable concluding statement |
| | May use rhetorical and persuasive strategies to engage the audience |
| **News articles**<br>**Opinion pieces**<br>**Editorials**<br>**Letters to the editor** | Include a headline, have a clear contention and use persuasive language (opinion pieces, editorials and letters to the editor) |
| | Use an authoritative tone |
| | News articles avoid first-person voice, use facts and evidence and present several perspectives and viewpoints |
| | Editorials use plural first-person voice and formal and sophisticated language |
| | Opinion pieces and letters to the editor use singular first-person voice, and their language style and register reflect their writer's character, purpose and audience |
| **Film scripts**<br>**Play scripts**<br>**Podcast scripts**<br>**Television scripts** | Consist mostly of dialogue, which may use sentence fragments, unconventional sentence structures and colloquial language to reflect everyday speech |
| | Include some stage directions with limited descriptions of action, set, props and actor instructions (play, television and film scripts) |
| | Divided into acts and scenes (play, television and film scripts) |
| | Dialogue reflects characterisation and cultural context |
| | Use a specific format (e.g. character names capitalised, stage directions italicised) |

If you write a text that would usually be delivered orally, you won't present it as an audio text. However, your transcript should show your understanding of how such texts are usually delivered (e.g. by including notes about music or sound effects and making the text easy to read aloud and to listen to).

# What you need to do

This section summarises everything you need to do to complete this SAC task.

## Prepare for the SAC task

In addition to the work you do in class for Unit 3 Outcome 2 Task 1, you can prepare by following the suggestions below.

### Read

One of the main aims of your writing is to explore the ideas suggested by the title and stimulus material you are likely to be given in connection with the Framework you are studying. This means that your text must show evidence that you have thought about these ideas in depth.

A common problem noted with student pieces in this area of the English course is that they lack depth and development of ideas. The best strategy to overcome this is to read widely.

Strong writers are avid readers. When you read a text that contains a good idea or example that you could incorporate into your writing, make notes about it. The more ideas you have to draw on, the stronger your piece of writing will be. Reading widely will also help you to develop your understanding of topics or issues you might like to write about. Become an expert on the topic on which you intend to write. For example, if you are writing about protest, learn some facts and statistics about the issue you will write about.

### Write

When writing, look for ways to extend, develop and deepen your ideas. Ask yourself *how* and *why* – that is, *how* (or in what ways) is an idea true or evident in the world, and *why* is this the case?

## Plan your original text

When choosing the focus of your written piece, keep in mind the following points.

**Develop the idea/s encapsulated in your given title, if there is one.** The title should provide the primary focus of your piece.

**Consider what you have learned from your mentor texts.** In your own writing, you don't have to use the specific ideas in the mentor texts you study, but you will have been thinking and talking a lot about the key idea that links them. This close consideration of an idea is likely to inspire and stimulate your own related but original ideas, which you could explore in your writing.

 

**Think about texts you have enjoyed or found valuable.** What did they have in common? Are you drawn to fantasy novels with detailed imaginary worlds? To texts that explain complex topics in accessible ways? To reflective pieces in which writers share their personal experiences? It is likely that you will enjoy writing about subjects and ideas similar to those you enjoy reading about.

**Choose an idea that genuinely interests you.** It's difficult to write effectively and engagingly about an idea or subject you're not interested in. Think about what excites you: it may be taking action to protect the natural environment, spending time with your friends, playing a sport, pondering the meaning of life or making TikToks with your cat. Your passion for your chosen idea will come across in your writing.

**Write what you know.** This advice, often given to writers, does not mean you shouldn't use your imagination or explore unfamiliar ideas. It just means that you should draw on the areas in which you have some expertise.

Perhaps you love to cook and know how to adapt recipes for different ingredients. Maybe you spend a lot of time at your local beach and have observed currents, tides and cloud formations.

You may have experienced a challenge (e.g. a serious injury, disappointment or bereavement) and learned about ways to cope. Maybe you are very knowledgeable about being a typical – yet unique – teenage student in an Australian secondary school!

Your piece does not have to focus only on your area of expertise, but your writing will benefit if you can draw on the things you understand well.

BRAINSTORM

1 **Write down three or four questions or ideas about the Framework that especially interest you. Brainstorm concepts for texts that each idea could lead to.**

2 **Make a list of forms and genres that you are very familiar with and for which you have a good understanding of features and conventions.**

3 **Think about previous pieces you have written and the feedback you have received. Is there a form of writing that you are particularly good at?**

4 **Consider which of the ideas you brainstormed for question 1 would work with one of the forms of writing you understand well and are capable of writing in. Once you have chosen an idea and form, check their suitability with your teacher.**

The plan for your text will depend on the form you have chosen to write in.

- If you are writing an imaginative piece, begin by listing the events of the plot in chronological order, even if your story will not present the events chronologically.
- If you are writing a persuasive piece, list the reasons for your viewpoint and the evidence you will use to support each reason. Decide in which order you will present your arguments.
- If you are writing a reflective piece, list the ideas you want to communicate in their order of importance.
- If you are writing an explanatory piece, list the steps, information or concepts you want to convey, in order from most basic or fundamental to most complex.

You can use a planning sheet like the one that follows to map your work. This template can also be useful when you're writing your reflective commentary.

| Key elements | Questions to consider | Notes |
|---|---|---|
| **Title** | What idea/s are encapsulated in the title (if given)? | |
| | What is your response to these ideas? | |
| | How will you shape your piece around the ideas? | |
| **Stimulus material** | If you have a choice of stimulus material to respond to, which item/s particularly stimulate your thinking? | |
| | How do the stimuli you have chosen to respond to connect to the ideas in your given title and the Framework you are studying? | |
| | How will you explore these ideas in your writing? | |
| **Ideas / aspects of the Framework** | What ideas or aspects of the Framework will you focus on? | |
| | Why will you focus on these ideas (i.e. what do you want to communicate)? | |

 

| Key elements | Questions to consider | Notes |
|---|---|---|
| **Form and genre** | What is the form of your piece? Why have you chosen that form? | |
| | How will the form help you explore or illuminate key aspects of the Framework? | |
| | What are the key features of the form and how will you use them? | |
| | What is the genre of your piece? Why have you chosen that genre? | |
| **Purpose and audience** | What is your main purpose in creating this piece? What do you want your audience to think or feel? | |
| | Who is your implied or intended audience? How will your response cater for that audience? | |
| **Language** | What adjectives could describe the language you will use? | |
| | What specific literary techniques will you use? | |
| | What effects are you aiming to create? | |
| **Mentor texts** | How will your piece demonstrate your study of the mentor texts? | |
| | What aspects of the mentor texts will you use in your piece? | |

WRITE

**Use the table above and on page 32 as a template to make notes about an original text you have written or plan to write.**

## Working with titles and stimulus material

In Section B of the end-of-Year-12 exam, you will be provided with:

- a title that you must use for your original text
- a set of stimuli (e.g. quotations, poems, images); you must respond to *at least one* in your original text.

It is likely that your SAC task will also involve working with a given title. The title will be open-ended, allowing you to take your writing in many possible directions.

For your written piece, you will be able to choose the:

- form
- target audience
- purpose
- focus.

Whatever choices you make regarding these elements, your piece must clearly show that you have engaged with and thought carefully about the title and the Framework ideas.

Mind maps and brainstorms are good ways to begin engaging with a given title. Try jotting down as many associations as you can think of. Keep in mind your Framework idea and try to draw connections between it and the title.

The quality and depth of your ideas are important aspects of this task, so even in a time-limited situation it's worth taking time to generate possible ideas to focus on. Select the one that offers the most scope for fruitful and original exploration in your text.

Next, consider the other aspects of the text that you must choose. For example, you might decide whether the idea would be best developed through a journal entry, a play script or a short story.

Whatever idea you decide to develop, you should plan it around the title and keep this title in mind as you write. Ways to respond to the title include:

- developing the idea in the title by exploring a different aspect of it in each paragraph
- incorporating words from the title in the text (although this alone is not enough to show your engagement with it)
- using the title as a symbol or motif in the text
- having someone in the text directly discuss or refer to the idea in the title
- opening or concluding with an explicit reflection on your interpretation of the title.

Once you have drafted your text, read it, keeping the title firmly in mind. Does the text clearly connect with and address the idea in the title? Will the person reading your work be able to identify the connections easily? If not, you might need to revise the text to make your engagement with the title clearer.

 

DISCUSS

**Work in a small group for this activity.**

1. **Each person in your group should create a title for a text. The titles should relate to the Framework you are studying and allow for a range of possible written responses.**
2. **Share your titles with the group. For each title, each member of the group should write down an idea for an original text that incorporates the title and allows for the exploration of Framework ideas.**
3. **Share your ideas with the group. Discuss which ones you think are especially interesting or potentially fruitful and the reasons for this.**
4. **Choose a title and text idea, either your own or one generated by another group member. Write a detailed plan for the text.**

To explore connections between any stimulus material you are presented with, the Framework and your own thoughts, you can use a similar process to the one for working with titles described on the opposite page.

Begin by selecting the stimulus item that most inspires or resonates with you. Make notes identifying the associations and emotions the stimulus evokes, the ideas it raises and your own responses to those associations, emotions and ideas.

Next, choose one or two of your ideas and brainstorm some possible texts you could develop.

Effective engagement with stimulus material can enrich your writing, adding depth and demonstrating your ability to think critically and creatively. However, you should integrate it naturally and purposefully, in ways that help you develop your ideas. Do not force references to stimuli into your work in awkward or inauthentic ways.

Below are several strategies for engaging with stimulus material in your writing.

- **Incorporation.** Use a quotation or a description of an image in your text.
- **Expression.** In an imaginative piece, have a character express a sentiment or idea equivalent to the idea expressed in the stimulus material.
- **Reflection.** Consider the implications of the stimulus and use them as a launching point for your piece.
- **Argument.** Use the stimulus as a basis for an argument: discuss its relevance to your Framework, and agree, disagree or propose a nuanced viewpoint. ⇨

- **Explanation.** Explain the meaning of the stimulus, focusing on its potential interpretations and considering their implications and significance.
- **Contrast.** If appropriate, draw a contrast or paradox between the stimulus and your main argument or narrative to develop interest and engagement.

The most important thing is to show your engagement with the Framework and the title you are given. The role of the stimulus material is to generate ideas relevant to these two elements.

WRITE

1 Create or find a set of three stimuli relevant to your Framework, consisting of:
   - a quotation or statement
   - an image
   - a poem or short extract from a text.

2 For each stimulus, brainstorm some ideas to explore in an original text. Then choose one of the ideas for each stimulus and outline a possible text you could write that explores that idea.

3 Use the table below as a template to record your stimuli, ideas and outlines from questions 1 and 2.

| Stimuli types | Stimuli | Ideas | Text outlines |
|---|---|---|---|
| Quotation or statement | | | |
| Image | | | |
| Poem or text extract | | | |

4 Choose one of the text outlines and write an original text of between 700 and 900 words based on the outline.

5 Write a short explanation of how you went about responding to the stimulus in completing question 4. How did the stimulus inspire you? What Framework ideas did it connect to?

 

## Developing a structure

'Structure' refers to the way your writing is organised; a strong structure helps to make a piece of writing clear and coherent. A structure requires an organising principle (a recognisable system or order), which could be:

- chronological (e.g. in a short story)
- moving from the general to the particular or from the particular to the general (e.g. in an explanatory piece)
- a development of an argument substantiating (giving proof or evidence for) a point of view (e.g. in a persuasive piece)
- the gradual unfolding of a point of view (e.g. in a reflective essay).

For example, a typical short story includes a plot arc with a structure that looks something like this:

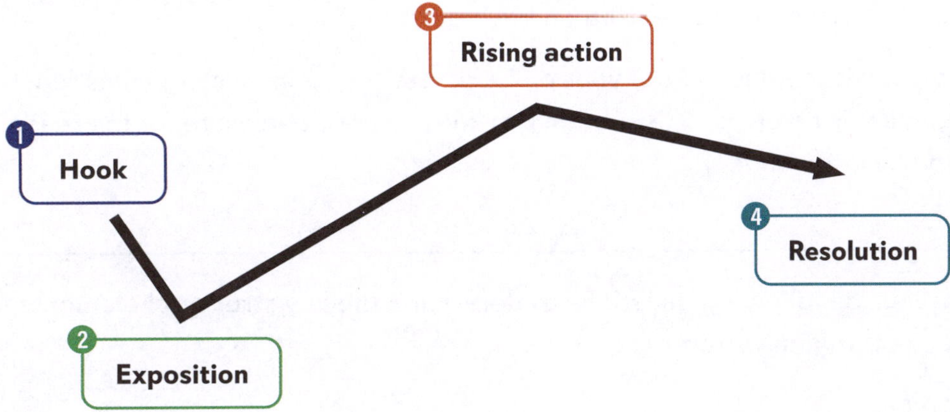


Even if you are not writing a short story, this structure is a useful guide to the way in which tension should rise and fall in your piece.

## Elements of structure

A *hook* is the first words of a text that are designed to grab the reader's attention and encourage them to continue reading. Here are two ideas for a hook in an original text.

- In a nonfiction text, a question or anecdote at the beginning can draw in readers.
- In a fictional text, beginning in medias res (in the middle of the action) can engage readers.

An *exposition* is the background information provided to a reader at the start of a text; this sets the scene for a story, an argument, an explanation or a reflection.

Your text should have a sense of movement. There should be a mystery to be solved, a question to be answered or a tension to be resolved. This should be established in the exposition.

The sense of movement should flow through the whole text:

- In a nonfiction text, an idea or argument should be developed.
- In a fictional text, characters should show some evidence of change or growth.

After you've hooked your readers and set the scene, you need to *escalate the action* or *develop your idea*. When doing this, keep these points in mind.

- In a nonfiction text (e.g. a speech or an opinion piece), you should identify key points of interest or change (e.g. revelation of important information or reasons).
- In a fictional text of this length, you won't have space for a complicated plot, so the action should be centred on one key event.

A *resolution* is the final part of your piece, where the main mystery, question, tension or argument is resolved. This section provides a sense of closure for the reader and ties up any loose ends.

PLAN

**Answer the following questions to determine the key structural elements in your piece of original writing.**

**Hook**

- **At what point, or with what engaging idea, will your piece begin?**
- **What will make the reader want to keep reading?**

**Exposition**

- **What background details or information will you include?**

**Rising action / development of an idea**

- **If you are writing a nonfiction text, how will you explore and expand on your main ideas?**
- **If you are writing a story or fictional text, what is the key event in the plot?**

**Resolution**

- **How will your piece conclude?**
- **What questions will be answered? Will anything be left unanswered?**
- **How will you ensure the reader feels a sense of closure and satisfaction?**

Your writing needs to hold the reader's interest. However, always keep in mind the *primary tasks* of the piece: to engage with the given title and chosen stimulus material, and to examine an idea connected to the Framework you are studying.

### Narrative voice

If you are writing a fictional narrative text such as a short story, think carefully about whose perspective it will be told from.

If your narrator is a character you have invented, you need a good understanding of the sort of person they are and the way in which they use language.

If your story is narrated in the third person (as though the narrator is an external observer of events), you still need to make decisions about their perspective. In this case, ask yourself the following questions about your narrator.

- Are they an **omniscient** narrator reporting objectively on events? Or are they **limited**, staying close to the perspective of a particular character?
- Do they have a **distinct personality** or an **attitude** towards characters and events?
- How does their personality or attitude affect the **language** they use?

Some text types, including most nonfiction texts, do not have a narrator. Instead, you express your ideas in your own voice.

Think carefully about the persona you want to project and the impression you want to convey to appeal to and engage with your intended audience. This means making careful language choices that consider your audience's prior knowledge about the topic or idea you are exploring, your audience's needs and preferences, and your purpose in writing.

# Writing an original text

This section contains advice and guidelines for producing an engaging, well-structured and fluent piece of writing.

## Elements of original texts

Key elements of original texts include the following.

### Engaging introductions

First impressions count. Make the first line of your written piece intriguing or memorable, and your audience will be keen to read the rest. Some tips on writing an engaging introduction are provided on the next page.

- If you are writing an imaginative piece, try starting in medias res (in the middle of the story).
- If you are writing a persuasive or an explanatory piece, you could begin with a surprising fact or statistic.
- If you are writing a reflective piece, you might open with a statement about something you have in common with your target audience.

## Exploring ideas in depth

As noted earlier, an important aspect of high-level original texts is their thoughtful exploration of the ideas encapsulated in the title and associated with the Framework. The list below discusses ways to do this.

- Have a bank of **interesting ideas** to draw on. Source these from your study of the Framework idea and mentor texts.
- Identify the **main ideas** you want to explore before you start writing. This will help you to retain a focus on them.
- Articulate the **key messages** you want to convey about the ideas you are exploring. No matter what form you are writing in, one aim should be to enrich and expand your audience's thinking about the piece's big ideas.
- Share **draft pieces** with others and ask them to identify the ideas and messages in your writing. If they are unable to do so, focus on this aspect of your work when rewriting.

## Developing complex characters

Most imaginative texts involve the development of interesting, believable characters. You should have a strong understanding of their backstories and natures.

Make notes about your characters' personality traits, important relationships, hopes and fears, dreams and goals, history and circumstances. You probably won't include all this information in your piece, but it will help you to present characters in a realistic way.

The following strategies will help you to develop convincing characters.

- **Drip-feed information.** Don't overload or bore the reader with a long summary of a character's appearance, background and personality. Instead, sprinkle these details through the narrative.
- **Include interesting details.** When you present information about a character, don't focus on broad details (e.g. their age, appearance or family relationships). Think about the small details that make them unique. Are they passionate about a particular musician or artist? Do they drag their feet when they walk? Do they overuse a particular word or phrase?

 

- **Carefully craft dialogue.** Your characters should speak in ways that reflect their personalities, ages, backgrounds and contexts. Different characters should speak in distinct ways. Dialogue is also a useful method to convey details about characters, rather than explaining this information in the narrative.
- **Develop your character/s.** Even in a short story, characters should grow or change in some way because of the events depicted.

Do not include too many characters in an original text. You won't have space to develop a large cast, and having lots of names is likely to make your piece confusing and unfocused.

## Show, don't tell

The short-story writer Anton Chekhov once said about writing, 'Don't tell me the moon is shining; show me the glint of light on broken glass.' You may have heard of the writing principle he was referring to: show, don't tell. This means that, rather than describing things such as mood, motivations and feelings, writers should allow readers to draw their own conclusions from, for instance, characters' actions, dialogue, descriptions of the surroundings or what is left unsaid.

The following paragraph is all *telling* and no *showing*. Everything is spelled out to the reader, leaving nothing for them to interpret or wonder about.

> Lincoln felt frustrated. He tried to talk to Serenity about why he wanted her to leave the police force, but she wouldn't listen. It seemed that the disagreement between this married couple would never be resolved. He started to cry, which only made Serenity angrier, because she felt his tears were a kind of moral blackmail.

Compare the paragraph above with the version below.

> Serenity clenched her fists and exhaled heavily. 'Lincoln, please –'. She walked over to the window and gazed out at the blue-green hills. Lincoln stared at her retreating back. A tear tracked down his cheek as he let out a sob. Serenity put her head in her hands and swore.

Do you see how the second paragraph is more interesting and engaging than the first? Readers are more likely to become engaged with a story if they are actively involved in considering the questions raised by the text.

What is Serenity pleading with Lincoln about? Why is he crying? What is going through Serenity's mind as she gazes out the window? Readers are made to feel as though the scene is happening right in front of them.

Using dialogue is an effective way to show rather than tell your audience something important about a character or the subject of a nonfiction text. Dialogue is interesting and gets readers involved, because it challenges them to work out things for themselves and have their own reactions, rather than being told things by the narrator.

REWRITE

**Find an original text that you have written previously and identify a paragraph that *tells* rather than *shows*. Rewrite the paragraph using the advice in this section.**

## Writing vividly

The vividness of your writing is an important element in this assessment. The guidelines below will help you to write in an engaging, fluent and sophisticated way, no matter what text type you are creating.

**Include sensory detail.** Don't just retell events. Describe the sights, sounds, smells and sensations associated with places, situations and people.

**Use varied and interesting vocabulary.** Avoid common, overused adjectives (e.g. 'good', 'nice', 'scary'). Use precise and evocative words (e.g. 'virtuous', 'benevolent', 'malicious').

Always consider the connotations (associations) of the words you use, as these convey relevant emotions and attitudes without you having to spell them out (allowing you to show rather than tell).

In addition, don't rely solely on adjectives to describe things. Strong nouns, verbs and adverbs can also help paint a vivid picture.

**Avoid clichés.** Come up with your own original metaphors and similes. Aim for unexpected, striking descriptions of places and characters.

**Avoid repetition and redundancy.** If you notice repeated words and phrases in your writing, delete them and find varied and interesting alternatives.

However, remember that repetition can be used purposefully to achieve specific effects. For example, the Rule of Three is a writing principle that suggests ideas presented in sets of three are memorable and effective. The well-known translation of a statement attributed to Julius Caesar – 'I came, I saw, I conquered' – uses this rule.

You can also use repetition to strengthen the structure of your piece. For example, many reflective essays or blog posts end by referring to an idea or statement introduced at the beginning.

 

**Don't overuse the passive voice.** 'The essay was written by Amara' is a sentence using the passive voice. It prioritises the *action* of the sentence (writing) over the *person performing* the action (Amara).

If you use lots of sentences in the passive voice, they can make your writing sound dull. Make sure some sentences are in the active voice (e.g. 'Amara wrote the essay').

**Don't try too hard to be 'literary'.** Good writing achieves a balance between lyrical and plain language.

Using large numbers of similes, metaphors, flowery descriptions and overly complex words will make your writing seem forced and it will be less effective. Imagery has more impact when it is used in moderation.

**Focus on small details.** Often, details make descriptions of people and events come alive. For example, rather than just stating that a big red car went by, be specific about the car's make and model, how much wear and tear it showed, how fast it was travelling and so on.

**Vary your sentence structures.** Your writing will be more fluent and interesting if you vary the beginnings of sentences, as well as the sorts of sentences you use.

Changing the lengths and complexity of sentences affects the pace of your writing. Short sentences can deliver concise, impactful statements or create effects like suspense, speed and humour. Long sentences can be useful for giving complex details, building an argument and slowing the pace and creating a relaxed rhythm.

REVIEW

**Find an original text that you have written previously. Referring to the guidelines in this section, annotate your original text to identify areas for improvement in your writing.**

Be careful with how much you try to do in your original text. Some poorer pieces of writing focus too much on recounting events or providing detailed background information at the expense of developing ideas.

## Improve your original text

You will have the opportunity to write and draft practice pieces before your SAC task. You can use these practice pieces to improve your writing skills by reflecting on and editing your work.

### Reflecting on your work

The following steps will help you to reflect on your writing and identify areas for improvement.

| | |
|---|---|
| Read your text. | Do this after you have had some time away from it and before you look at your teacher's feedback. Which aspects do you think work well, and which do not? What would you do differently next time? |
| Identify the main areas for improvement. | Do you need to work on structuring effective pieces in particular forms, on building narrative tension, on clearly presenting an argument, or on something else? |
| Reflect on your development as a writer. | Make notes on your teacher's thoughts, as well as your own, about your work. Consider what you learned through this writing task and the aspects you found especially challenging. Refer to these notes before your next attempt at writing an original text. |

### Editing your work

You can use a checklist like the one that follows to edit your work. Complete the checklist after each draft of a practice piece. Aim to tick every cell of the final column.

| What you should check | First draft | Second draft | Third draft |
|---|---|---|---|
| **Form and focus** | | | |
| The main idea you are exploring and its connection to the title and Framework are clear. | | | |
| The purpose (or purposes) of the text is clear. | | | |
| The structure and features of the form have been used appropriately. | | | |
| The piece has a clear beginning, middle and end, as well as a pattern of rising and falling tension or development of an argument or idea. | | | |

 

| What you should check | First draft | Second draft | Third draft |
|---|---|---|---|
| **Links to the key idea and mentor texts** | | | |
| The text shows an in-depth understanding and thoughtful consideration of the ideas connected to the Framework. | | | |
| The text demonstrates clear engagement with the given title and its ideas. | | | |
| The text clearly responds to at least one piece of stimulus material in a thoughtful way. | | | |
| The language and other features of the mentor texts have been drawn on in a purposeful way. | | | |
| **Language** | | | |
| The voice is consistent, engaging and appropriate to the chosen narrator or the writer. | | | |
| The style (formality and type of language used) is consistent and appropriate to the purpose, form and audience. | | | |
| Literary devices (e.g. figurative language, imagery) have been used to achieve specific effects. | | | |
| Each sentence starts with a capital letter and ends with concluding punctuation. | | | |
| Grammar, punctuation and spelling are correct throughout (unless varied to achieve a particular purpose). | | | |

1. **For each paragraph of your piece, identify the idea/s it develops and how it does this. If you find this difficult, consider how you might strengthen your presentation and development of ideas.**
2. **Highlight three sentences you are proud of. What do you like about them?**
3. **Change or edit three other sentences so that they have more of the qualities of the sentences you highlighted in question 2.**
4. **Replace three vocabulary choices with more precise or evocative options.**
5. **Swap pieces with a partner. Identify evidence of your partner's engagement with the title and the Framework, as well as ways they could improve this.**

## Common mistakes and tips for top responses

The table below outlines some common mistakes made in original texts and explains how to fix them.

| Mistakes | Solutions |
|---|---|
| Telling rather than showing | Read over your work, looking for words or phrases that can indicate you are telling rather than showing (e.g. 'then', 'next', 'they felt', 'they were [emotion]').<br><br>Replace these with descriptions that imply a character's state of mind or behaviour (e.g. change 'Nat felt disappointed' to 'Nat's shoulders slumped'). |
| Not having a clear structure | Look at the summary table of forms on pages 28–9 and check that you have used the features of the form you are writing in.<br><br>Identify the hook, exposition, rising tension and resolution in your piece. If you can't, you might need to rework it. |
| Not showing clear links to the title and Framework | Make a dot-point list of the ways in which your piece draws on the title and Framework.<br><br>Swap pieces with a partner and identify in each other's piece the connections between the text and the title and Framework. If your partner can't identify many connections or if they identify very different connections from those you intended, you should revise your work to build in clearer links. |
| Not presenting a polished piece of writing | The text should contain well-crafted sentences and varied and effective vocabulary. Even in a time-limited situation, allow approximately five minutes to read over your work and check for clunky or unclear expression, and spelling and punctuation errors. |

Keep in mind the following advice for producing a high-level original text.

- **Brainstorm multiple ideas** in the planning phase. Your first idea is not necessarily the best.
- **Choose an idea** that has a strong and clear connection to the title and the Framework you are studying.
- **Choose a form** that you are familiar with and comfortable writing in.
- **Maintain a clear focus**, as you won't have time to write thousands of words, present a highly complex argument or develop a large cast of characters. Pinpoint the main idea/s you want to explore, your primary purpose and your target audience, and concentrate on these elements.

 

- **Take time to edit your work**; read it to ensure it makes sense and that your writing is fluent. Rewrite inelegant sentences; replace dull or imprecise vocabulary choices with more interesting ones; and correct spelling, punctuation and grammatical errors.

# REFLECTIVE COMMENTARIES

For Unit 3 Outcome 2 Task 2, you must explain your writing processes in a reflective commentary of approximately 400 words.

You may write in the first or the third person. You may use the notes from your planning (see pages 32–3) as the basis for your reflective commentary.

## What you need to know

This section summarises everything you need to know to successfully complete this SAC task.

### Performance descriptors

Your reflective commentary will be assessed against a set of performance descriptors. The 'very high' performance descriptors – which describe a response likely to receive between 17 and 20 marks out of a maximum of 20 – are reproduced in the left-hand column in the table below. The right-hand column presents advice on how to achieve this.

| 'Very high' performance descriptors | What you need to do |
| --- | --- |
| Composes a detailed account of the writing processes attempted and/or implemented through the experience of creating a text, and reflects on other writing processes. | Be thorough and specific in explaining your writing choices. |
| | Quote from your text where appropriate to indicate where and why you made specific choices. |
| Explains in detail how authorial choices around structures, language features, vocabulary and conventions interact to engage with ideas. | Clearly articulate the ideas your text is exploring. |
| | Focus on how your choices helped you to explore and develop ideas. |
| Connects precise language, register, structure and ideas to reflect on the writing processes. | Be specific about your text's target audience and purpose, remembering that there may be more than one of each. |
| | Draw connections between your choices and the ideas you are exploring for the text's purpose and audience. |

## What you need to do

This section summarises everything you need to do to complete this SAC task.

The aim of your reflective commentary is to explain how you created your text/s and why you made the choices you did. Focus on explaining how your decisions relating to your original text allowed you to effectively explore and develop ideas connected with the title and Framework.

Your reflective commentary should explain:

- how you engaged with and explored the idea/s encapsulated in the given title
- other connected ideas you chose to explore and the reasons for this
- how you responded to any stimulus material
- why you chose the specific form and how you used its features to explore ideas and achieve your purpose
- the language features and vocabulary you used and the reasons for this
- how you drew from the mentor texts as examples of strong writing
- how you think your audience might respond.

You can use the following sentence starters in your commentary.

| Reflective commentary sentence starters |
| --- |
| The primary purpose of my text is ... |
| The title prompted my exploration of ... |
| In my piece I aimed to ... by ... |
| I chose to incorporate [stimulus material] because ... I did this by ... |
| It was important to me that my audience felt ... so I used ... |
| I took inspiration from the mentor text when I ... |
| One of the language features I used was ... The intended effect of this is ... |
| Throughout the piece, I chose to ... |
| Overall, I encapsulated the atmosphere of ... |
| Here, I experimented with ... by ... |

 

## Sample reflective commentary

The reflective commentary below accompanied a text for the Framework 'Writing about personal journeys'.

> The title I was presented with – 'Journey of Discovery' – prompted images of uncharted territories and adventure, which connected with the Framework of personal journeys to inspire me to write a fictional biography about an unconventional explorer. The character I created was a timid office worker who accidentally becomes involved in a rescue mission while on holiday. This unexpected situation forces them to display courage they hadn't known they possessed. Their physical journey prompts and reflects a journey of self-development; their 'discovery' is of both a place and of themselves. The biography form allowed me to trace this journey in a linear way and to take an objective perspective that helped to deliver a clear message about challenging oneself.
>
> My main purpose was to express but I also wanted to persuade my target audience of educated adult readers interested in travel stories to look a little deeper into the places they visit and the reasons for their travels. Harvey, my main character, gives little thought, at first, to the resort staff who make his holiday so idyllic and has no desire to venture beyond the resort to see more of the country he has journeyed to, until he is forced to by a natural disaster.
>
> I took inspiration from the stimulus image of a series of stepping stones in a lake, leading to a distant horizon. It suggests that there is no way of knowing one's limits until you are tested. I also drew on Amy Duong's memoir, 'The Red Plastic Chair is a Vietnamese Cultural Institution, and My Anchor', with its motif of the red plastic chair. I used a plastic sun lounge to symbolise the artificiality of the resort environment and the ignorance of many who visit them, like Harvey.
>
> As appropriate to a biography, I used a mostly formal, neutral tone, as though reporting facts. However, I also used some sophisticated and lyrical language to explore lessons I hoped readers would take from Harvey's story; for example, in the references to the 'light of understanding' that suffuses Harvey like the dawning sun after the earthquake.
>
> I used shorter sentences to convey factual information about Harvey, such as his age and job. I also used short sentences and fragments to convey the sudden disruption of the earthquake. However, I used longer descriptive sentences, with adjectives such as 'sheltered' and 'paradisical', to describe the resort. I also used longer, more complex sentences when exploring the changes in Harvey following his journey as these allowed me to express more complex ideas in a nuanced and precise way.

REVIEW

**Annotate the sample reflective commentary above, identifying three strengths and two areas for improvement.**

Chapter 03

UNIT 4 OUTCOME 2 (TASK 1):

# Analyses of argument and language

For Unit 4 Outcome 2 Task 1, you must write an analysis of the use of argument and persuasive language a text that presents a point of view on an issue. The text will include written and visual, audio or audiovisual material, and will have appeared in the media since 1 September of the previous year.

The analysis is worth 40 marks. The suggested length of the analysis is 700 to 900 words.

## What you need to know

This section summarises everything you need to know to successfully complete this SAC task.

### Performance descriptors

Your analysis will be assessed against a set of performance descriptors. The 'very high' performance descriptors – which describe a response likely to receive between 33 and 40 marks out of a maximum of 40 – are reproduced in the left-hand column in the following table. The right-hand column presents advice on how to achieve this.

| 'Very high' performance descriptors | What you need to do |
|---|---|
| Examines critically how the author guides an audience by use of strategic sequencing of argument. | Pay attention to the order in which the writer presents their reasons and consider why they have ordered them in this way. |
| | Consider other structuring strategies (e.g. subheadings, pullout boxes, paragraphing). |
| Examines subtle connections between language features and vocabulary and the implications of these features in relation to persuading the intended audience. | Think about the associations and connotations of the writer's language choices, focusing on the intended effects, including emotional responses, they aim to generate. |
| | Identify the specific intended audience/s, thinking about how the writer's choices are intended to affect the audience in the context of the text. |

| 'Very high' performance descriptors | What you need to do |
|---|---|
| Examines pivotal aspects of the text and the role of inference and its relation to persuasive intent. | Look beyond the literal meaning of the writer's words to identify the implications of what they are saying. |
| | Consider the ideas the writer is connecting to and the associations they are aiming to raise for the reader. |
| Examines subtle connections between visual(s) and the implications of these features in relation to persuading the intended audience. | Use metalanguage related to visual material (e.g. 'focus', 'framing', 'style'). |
| | Draw connections between the visual material and the written text. |
| Examines subtle connections between audio and/or audio visual features and the implications of these features in relation to persuading the intended audience. | Use appropriate metalanguage for analysing audio and/or audiovisual elements of a text. |
| | Consider the ways in which these features are utilised by the text creator to evoke specific emotions and responses in a particular audience. |
| | Make links between these features and the written text, considering how they work together to position the audience. |
| Composes a complex exposition that examines and clarifies how strategic sequencing of argument guides the intended audience to a particular position.<br>Creates a fluent response using appropriate language and precise metalanguage to examine the text's persuasive intent. | Consider the development of the argument. How does the author aim to lead the reader along a certain path to a particular conclusion? |
| | Use vocabulary related to structure, such as 'having established', 'by beginning with' and 'in concluding'. |
| | Use precise analytical vocabulary that pinpoints the writer's intentions. |
| | Vary your sentence structures and vocabulary choices to improve fluency. |

## Key knowledge and skills

Knowing the important concepts and metalanguage associated with this area of study is vital for success in this SAC task.

An *argument* is a point of view supported by *reasons* and relevant *evidence*. A crucial part of a writer's argument is their *contention*: the central idea or opinion they express. Linked to the contention is the writer's *purpose*: what they want their intended *audience* to do, think or feel. To achieve this, a writer shapes their text to suit their intended audience's needs and preferences, considering the *context* of the issue and publication.

## Contention

Your first step is to identify the writer's contention (the central idea or opinion expressed in the text). The contention may be:

- encapsulated in the headline or title of the text
- stated in the opening paragraph
- stated in the concluding paragraph
- implied through reasons and language choices.

## Structure and approach

Next, identify the basic structure of the argument. Ask yourself the following.

- How do the points of argument support and develop the writer's contention?
- In what order are supporting reasons presented (e.g. most important to least important or least important to most important)?
- Is a solution given? (A solution is often the strongest point of an argument.)
- Are alternative viewpoints considered? Does the writer agree with or rebut any aspects of the alternative viewpoints?
- Does the writer create a dichotomy (e.g. 'good' versus 'evil', practicality versus idealism, logic versus emotion)?

Consider also the writer's overall approach to the topic.

- Do they base their argument primarily on ethical, practical or financial considerations?
- Do they aim to appeal primarily to the reader's emotions, reason or self-interest?

After identifying important structural elements and the writer's main approach, divide the text into three or four main sections. You can analyse these in turn in your body paragraphs. Each topic sentence should identify the point of the argument you are analysing and how the argument is sequenced – that is, how each point flows on from the previous point and supports the writer's contention.

## Tone

Form, audience and purpose influence the tone of a text; for example, consider how the friendly and confiding tone of an influencer's Instagram post differs from the formal, measured tone of a newspaper editorial. When analysing tone:

- identify the tone using a precise descriptive word
- identify some words and phrases in the text that contribute to this tone
- explain the intended effect of the tone on the target audience.

Remember that a writer's or speaker's tone can change over the course of a text. A change of tone often signals a change in argument – for example, a shift from targeting the audience members' emotions to appealing to their sense of reason.

READ

**Below is a list of words commonly used to describe tone. For each word, find an example in a persuasive text.**

aggressive angry annoyed anxious concerned defiant

disappointed earnest encouraging firm friendly hopeful

hostile matter-of-fact measured optimistic outraged passionate

reproachful sarcastic serious sorrowful sympathetic worried

## Argument and language techniques

When analysing a writer's use of language, try to identify:

- the target audience's anticipated emotional response (how the writer wants the audience to feel)
- the needs or desires being appealed to or manipulated and how
- key words that aim to trigger the emotional response
- what the writer wants the audience to believe or think.

If you can refer to a particular persuasive technique using appropriate metalanguage (e.g. 'analogy', 'inclusive language'), then you should. However, it is not necessary to do so to analyse an example of persuasive language; the focus should always be on the writer's intended effect on their specific audience.

An important aspect of high-level analytical essays is their concentration on particular words and phrases. To do this, identify examples of especially persuasive language in the text and note:

- their associations and connotations
- the image they are intended to paint in the audience's mind
- the intended emotional effect of the word choice.

When analysing persuasive language, explain the intended emotional response of the audience and the object of the emotion (e.g. 'Parents are positioned to *feel contempt* for the *school administration*').

**Some common argument strategies and persuasive language techniques you should be familiar with are listed below. For each technique, find an example in a persuasive text.**

analogy anecdote appeal to being modern / up to date appeal to fear appeal to financial interest appeal to justice association cause-and-effect logic cliché connotation dichotomy exaggeration generalisation hyperbole inclusive language metaphor precedent repetition rhetorical question simile slippery-slope argument

If you detect patterns of language use, comment on them; e.g. 'The writer uses a series of anecdotes in order to …' or 'The writer uses exaggeration and repetition to stimulate [a particular emotion]'.

## Visual material

The written text will likely be accompanied by some form of visual material, such as a cartoon, drawing, photograph, chart or graph. *You must analyse the visual material*, linking it to the written text. This section describes some common types of visual materials.

**Photographs** tend to validate a point of view, as they are perceived to be objective and reliable. Remember, though, that they are carefully composed to convey a point of view.

**Cartoons** often target the audience's sense of humour to stimulate reflection on an issue. They may also be used to ridicule or arouse contempt, often by exaggerating certain features of the person being mocked or elements of the issue. Cartoons always express a point of view.

**Graphs and charts**, like photographs, are often viewed as objective forms of evidence, but the data is always carefully selected, and graphs and charts are arranged to convey a particular angle on an issue. Information may be emphasised or omitted to support a particular view.

You do not have to analyse every aspect of the visual material. Focus on the key elements and what they symbolise or convey. What emotions do they target? How do they aim to steer the audience's response?

 

### Audio and audiovisual material

You might be asked to analyse audio or audiovisual elements of a text. Consider the following.

The way in which the spoken elements of an audio or audiovisual text are delivered will affect how the audience responds to the main message. Consider the *appearance* and *body language* of the speaker, presenter or actor. Their clothing, hairstyle, accessories and props will be carefully selected to appeal to their intended audience. They might use gestures such as pointing for emphasis or thumping a hand on the lectern to show conviction. Their facial expressions will also convey their attitude towards the topic.

*Tone, pacing* and *pitch* are important aspects of a speaker's delivery. Tone refers to the emotional quality of the voice; it can be used to create a particular mood or emotion in the listener, and usually matches the tone of the speaker's language. Pacing refers to the speed and rhythm of the message, and can be used to create a sense of urgency or importance. The pitch (high or low) or volume of a speaker's voice can also be used to convey emotion or emphasise a point. *Music* and *sound effects* may be used to create particular moods or evoke certain emotions in the listener.

In an audiovisual text, cinematography, editing and special effects contribute to the way the message is 'packaged' and delivered to the audience. The *colour scheme* will affect the mood or atmosphere of the text. For instance, bright colours can evoke joy, while dark colours might convey seriousness. Similarly, *lighting* may be bright or dim, to convey an uplifting or a sombre perspective on an issue.

# What you need to do

This section summarises everything you need to do to complete this SAC task.

## Prepare for the SAC task

In addition to the work you do in class for Unit 4 Outcome 2 Task 1, you can also prepare by following the suggestions below.

- **Revise text types.** Ensure you are familiar with the features of a range of persuasive text types, so that you are well prepared to analyse how writers use these features for particular effects (e.g. a letter to the editor is written in the first person and often uses emotive language designed to target the reader's feelings, while an editorial is more formal and impersonal, which can help to convey authority).

- **Practise identifying the key elements of persuasive texts.** Draw a table like the one below and make brief notes on the main elements of a variety of persuasive texts.

| Main elements | Text 1 | Text 2 | Text 3 |
|---|---|---|---|
| Text title, text type, writer and place of publication | | | |
| Contention | | | |
| Main supporting reasons | | | |
| Main tone | | | |
| Important persuasive techniques | | | |
| Key quotations | | | |
| Visual, audio or audiovisual material | | | |

- **Write practice analytical sentences.** Select three elements for each text you identified above, and write one sentence for each element explaining its intended effect on the reader.

## Plan your analysis

Before you begin writing your analysis, you should annotate the text, identifying the main elements and examples that you want to analyse. Then organise your notes into a brief plan.

Your first step should always be to read any background information provided. This will give you key details about the text, such as the issue, the writer's qualifications or connection to the issue, and the place the text was published or presented.

### Annotating the text

To annotate a text for analysis, you should complete the tasks below.

- **Read the background information carefully.**
- **Identify the issue, contention, target audience and purpose** of the text.

 

- **Highlight key persuasive words and phrases.**
- **Note the main tone** and any changes in tone.
- **Make brief notes on any visual, audio or audiovisual material** and how it supports or challenges the points of view in the written text.
- **Use coloured pens or highlighters to identify multiple examples of a persuasive strategy or technique, or words and phrases that aim to provoke a particular emotion.** Use different colours for different strategies or techniques.

The following annotated text excerpt, from an opinion piece published in *The Sydney Morning Herald*, shows how you might highlight and make notes around a text to identify the elements you will analyse in your essay.

**Dear fellow pedestrians, keep to the left, you drongos**

Clare Heaney

When I'm walking along the footpath, I'm a firm lefty. Keep to the left as best as you can unless you're overtaking or there is some impediment.

I'm not sure if it is me, or something I've noticed more since the lockdowns, but people seem increasingly oblivious to this idea.

The other day as I made my way down the Paris end of Collins Street to a show, I was met with a throng of 'meanderthals' all heading towards me on what is a comparatively wide street.

They had plenty of room to walk to their left. I had to come to a standstill or sideswipe a shopfront. It's a small thing, but in a chain of small things, from not being able to get a seat on public transport because someone has their backpack on it, listening to people rabbit on in crowded places while they conduct a video call and not being able to get off a tram before people board, it just adds up.

It's easy as we age to dismiss ourselves as 'invisible', but people of all ages with dodgy knees and less obvious ailments can't so easily accommodate sudden directional changes as people weave in and out. Spare a thought for the elderly, people living with disabilities, the pregnant and the sight-impaired amid this free for all.

Annotations:

- Contention (fellow pedestrians, keep to the left)
- Humorous & exasperated tone suggests writer's overall approach (you drongos)
- Issue = footpath etiquette (Keep to the left as best as you can)
- Suggests problem is widespread & growing (people seem increasingly oblivious to this idea)
- Anecdotal evidence (I made my way down the Paris end of Collins Street)
- Play on words (merging perjorative terms 'meandering' and 'Neanderthals') draws attention to the irritating behaviour; this creates associations with lack of culture/sophistication ('meanderthals')
- Concedes a possible objection from readers: issue is minor; rebuts by pointing out accumulation of selfish behaviours generally (It's a small thing)
- Appeals to readers' compassion (people of all ages with dodgy knees and less obvious ailments)
- Connotations of chaos & selfishness – evokes alarm (free for all)

Allow yourself five to ten minutes to annotate the text. Identifying persuasive elements to analyse is an important step, but you need to spend the bulk of your time writing your analysis.

ANNOTATE

1 **Work with a partner to find a persuasive text on a contemporary issue. Print a copy of the text for each of you.**

2 **Annotate the text according to the guidelines on pages 56–7.**

3 **Swap texts with your partner and compare your annotations. Did you identify similar persuasive elements? While there is no single correct way to analyse a text, comparing your work with a partner's can alert you to important aspects of a text you might have missed.**

## Creating a plan

Use your annotations as the basis for your plan and decide how you will order your analysis of the different elements. The best approach is to focus on one main point of the writer's argument in each body paragraph.

Look for three or four main points in the text. Then look for examples of persuasive language used to present each point. Make sure you analyse all the main arguments.

Remember that you are not expected to analyse every reason, piece of evidence or example of persuasive language in the text. Instead, you need to be selective.

Here are some tips to help you select elements to analyse.

- Choose techniques and/or language that **you feel confident analysing** and that **contribute significantly to the overall impact** of the text.
- Select examples of language use that are **representative of how the writer uses language** at a particular point in the text (e.g. if three anecdotes are presented, analyse one rather than all of them).
- **If you can't explain** an example's intended effect on the reader, don't discuss it.

 

# Writing an analysis of argument and language

This section contains advice, guidelines and word banks for writing your analysis of argument and language.

## Elements of analytical texts

Key elements of media text analyses include the following.

### Introduction

Drawing on any background information and the text itself, your introduction should identify the:

- writer, title, text type and place of publication
- issue and any relevant contextual information
- writer's contention, purpose and intended audience
- main persuasive approaches or strategies used by the writer.

The table on the next page gives you some sentence starters that can be used in your introduction.

| Introduction sentence starters |
|---|
| Contending that ..., the writer then ... |
| The writer quickly establishes their contention that ... |
| The writer's claim that ... encapsulates their contention. |
| In an inflammatory tone, the writer declares that ... |
| The point of view presented by [name of writer] is shaped by the context of... |
| Adopting an adversarial position, the writer argues that ... |
| Arguing from a position of principle, the writer asserts that ... |
| [Name of writer] takes a considered, logical approach with the aim of influencing the reader to ... |
| Aiming to appeal primarily to the reader's ..., the writer states that ... |
| The use of ... positions the reader to share the writer's viewpoint that ... |
| Published in ..., for an audience consisting primarily of ..., the text presents ... |
| Addressing the dual audiences of ... and ..., [name of writer] contends that ... |

## Body paragraphs

The body of the analysis should contain three to five paragraphs. In each body paragraph, you should do the following.

- **Begin with a clear topic sentence** indicating the focus of the paragraph (i.e. the point of argument or persuasive strategies you will be analysing).
- **Present evidence from the text**, including quotations.
- **Suggest how these examples are intended to create effects** on the reader.

Avoid generic explanations of how devices work (such as 'The speaker cites an authority figure to arouse the listener's confidence' or 'The writer uses inclusive language to make the audience feel included'). Instead, relate your explanation to the specific example. For instance, you could write, 'The writer quotes Professor X, an expert in secondary education, in order to gain the trust of the parents in his proposal to add an extra year to secondary education' or 'By quoting Professor X, the writer hopes to gain the reader's trust, since parents reading this would tend to respect the opinions of an educational expert'.

Also, be wary of statements such as 'The writer says' or 'The writer states'. These usually result in nothing more than a restatement of the content, identifying *what* the writer says rather than *how* and *why* they are saying it.

One way to ensure that your analysis stays focused on the intended effects of the writer's argument and language choices is to learn some sentence stems like the ones below. Supply the missing words to relate your statements to the specific content of the text you are analysing.

| Body paragraph sentence stems |
|---|
| When the writer uses the phrase '[quotation from text]', they want the audience to feel [emotion] about [something]. |
| The expression '[quotation from text]' encourages the audience to view [something] as [adjective]. |
| The words '[quotation from text]' position the audience to feel/believe/do [something]. |

Do not put forward your opinion on the issue or evaluate the effectiveness of the arguments. This means you should avoid statements like 'The audience will feel [emotion]'. Instead, say 'The audience *is meant to feel* [emotion]' or 'The audience *is positioned to believe* [concept]'.

 

It can also be helpful to learn some analytical sentence stems, patterns and starters. A basic formula for writing analytical sentences is shown below, with examples.

| Who | Does | What | To make | Whom | Do what |
|---|---|---|---|---|---|
| The writer | uses | statistics | to encourage | the reader | to believe their claims |
| The speaker | employs | exaggeration | to position | the listeners | to feel anxious |
| Ms Jaya | cites | an anecdote | to incline | the audience | to sympathise with her |
| The policy document | includes | an emotive case study | to persuade | voters | to support the government's approach |
| The pamphlet | appeals to | the reader's sense of justice | to prompt | them | to feel outraged |

The following tables list sentence starters that can be used to write about specific aspects of persuasive texts.

| Persuasive technique sentence starters |
|---|
| Reminding the reader of past events is aimed at triggering associations of … |
| By introducing a controversial example, the writer positions the reader to … |
| The use of colourful language predisposes the reader to … |
| Highlighting conflict in the debate, the writer hopes that the audience will respond by … |
| References to experts / scientific findings / statistics are intended to lend credibility to the writer's argument, inclining the reader to … |
| The use of a stereotypical example contributes to the effect of … |
| Highly emotive language, such as …, positions the reader to accept/reject … |
| With the accumulation of examples and statistics, the writer seeks to convince the audience that … |
| The deliberately explosive opening pressures the target audience of … to accept … |
| Reference to the well-known authority of … suggests that … |
| Using statistics to support their point, the writer hopes to add legitimacy to their position that … |

⇨

| Persuasive technique sentence starters |
| --- |
| The writer establishes that … by deriding the opposing viewpoint, hoping to provoke the reader's … |
| Through repetition of the word/phrase '[quotation]', the writer seeks to coerce the reader into believing that … |
| In associating … with …, the writer aims to instil trust in their position. |
| With a series of rhetorical questions, the writer aims to appeal to … |
| The writer flatters supporters of the idea by referring to them as … |
| The word/phrase '[quotation]' has connotations of …, having the effect of … |
| When the writer uses the word/phrase '[quotation]', they want the audience to feel … |
| By using …, the writer intends the audience to understand … and therefore to believe … |
| The writer targets the reader's … by … |
| The reader is expected to respond to … by … |

| Tone sentence starters |
| --- |
| The sombre tone established by the writer is intended to highlight … |
| Designed to provoke anxiety in the audience, the tone is … |
| In a mocking tone, the writer … |
| The writer's forthright tone is created by using short, sharp sentences and such words/phrases as '[quotation]'. |
| Using evocative language, the writer establishes a … tone aimed at … |
| Words/phrases such as '[quotation]' and '[quotation]' contribute to a sarcastic tone that expresses the writer's disdain for … |
| The tone shifts as the writer goes on to discuss … |

 

| Language style sentence starters |
|---|
| The writer's use of a formal style and extensive research findings reinforces their credentials as … |
| By addressing the target audience formally/informally, the writer establishes a sense of … with the reader. |
| The chatty and colloquial language immediately draws the reader into … |
| The writer uses a relaxed style and numerous familiar examples that position the audience to engage with … |

| Visual , audio and audiovisual material sentence starters |
|---|
| The sombre colours of the set have associations with …, encouraging the viewer to feel … |
| The thick, bold lines of the illustration, together with the blunt caption, communicate a direct message to the audience that … |
| Placed prominently on the page, the stark photograph positions the reader to … |
| The grim humour of the cartoon aims at provoking a … response. |
| The presenter highlights … through their dramatic body language and exaggerated facial expressions. |
| The writer aims to reinforce the audience's [emotion] through the [key feature] of the illustration, which … |
| This point is reinforced through the speaker's tone, which positions the reader to feel [emotion] because … |

WRITE

1 **For each of the tables on pages 61–3, create one extra sentence starter of your own.**

2 **Choose one of the sentence starters from each table on pages 61–3 and use it to write an analytical sentence about a persuasive text of your choosing.**

## Conclusion

In your conclusion, make sure you follow these steps.

- Identify the overall approach of the text.
- Summarise the main persuasive strategies used by the writer to achieve their purpose.
- Draw the discussion to a logical close.

You can use the following sentence starters in conclusions.

| Conclusion sentence starters |
| --- |
| Having established …, the writer concludes by … |
| Reflecting the context in which they are writing as well as the make-up of their target audience, the writer takes a/an [adjective] approach to conveying their point of view. |
| Relying primarily on [technique] and [technique], the writer aims to lead the reader to support their proposed solution to [issue]. |
| In summary, the writer takes a logical approach to the issue, demonstrated by … |
| As has been shown, the main emotions targeted by the writer are … |
| By creating a dichotomy and employing a calm and measured tone, the writer aims to … |
| The writer's use of humour and hyperbole throughout positions the reader to … |

# Improve your analysis

You will have the opportunity to write and draft practice analyses of media texts before your SAC task. The following advice could help you to improve your analysis from a 'medium' to a 'very high' performance.

## Understanding of the argument

You must show that you understand the writer's argument and how they have constructed it. Here are some tips.

- **Check that you have referred to the writer's purpose** and how this affects their selection of reasons to support their argument.
- **Comment on the structure of the text**, which is the order that the writer presents their reasons, where and whether they explicitly state their contention, and whether they use features like headings or subheadings and visual material such as graphs, charts or tables, and/or audio or audiovisual material such as embedded video or voiceover.

- **Show your understanding of the multiple factors that affect how the writer shapes their argument** (e.g. the text type, the audience being targeted and the context in which the text is written and published).

## Analysis

You must *analyse* the text, looking at both individual elements and how they work together. Here are some tips.

- **Analyse not only the most obvious persuasive strategies or examples but also some more implicit or less obvious ones**, to show that you understand the subtleties of the argument and the way in which it is presented.
- **Comment on how certain persuasive strategies or examples of persuasive language work together** to achieve a combined or cumulative effect (e.g. by evoking a similar emotion).
- **Select particular words and phrases to analyse closely**, considering their connotations and associations as well as why the writer selected those particular words rather than others.
- **Identify persuasive techniques by name, if you can do so**, but remember that analysing the intended effect is always more important than correctly naming a technique.

## Written language

It is important that you use language and punctuation precisely and correctly. Here are some tips.

- **Read your work** to check that you have used a variety of sentence structures and lengths.
- **Consider using semicolons and colons** in addition to commas, to vary your punctuation.
- **Check spelling and grammar carefully**, including spellings of the writers' names and quotations from the text.
- **Avoid repeating stems** like 'The writer says' and vocabulary like 'effect', 'persuade' and 'feel'. Replace repeated words with more precise and interesting synonyms. Some possible alternatives to common words and phrases are shown on the next page.

## Expanding your vocabulary

You might find, when re-reading your analysis, that you have overused certain words or phrases. Your writing will be improved by replacing some of these with alternatives like those shown in the word bank on the next page.

| Common words and phrases | Words or phrases with similar meanings |
|---|---|
| argues | asserts, considers, contends, contests, demonstrates, expounds, maintains, posits |
| persuades | compels, convinces, influences, leads, manipulates, positions, predisposes, pressures, sways |
| supports | advocates, backs, champions, endorses, promotes |
| rejects | challenges, disapproves of, dismisses, negates, rebuts, repudiates |
| emphasises | accentuates, highlights, places weight on, stresses, underlines |
| aims | aspires, attempts, endeavours, hopes, intends, means |
| opinion | argument, case, contention, point of view, position, proposition |
| effect | consequence, impact, impression, influence, result |
| also | additionally, as well, furthermore, in addition, moreover |
| on the other hand | alternatively, conversely, however, in opposition to, whereas |

REVISE

1. **Use a thesaurus to identify more words and phrases that you can use in an analysis.**
2. **Read a draft of an analysis you have written. Circle or highlight three words or phrases that you have repeated. (If you can't find three examples of repetition, identify three words or phrases you think could be replaced with more precise vocabulary choices.)**
3. **Use a thesaurus to find suitable alternatives for the words or phrases you highlighted in question 2. Make sure the replacement words still convey your intended meaning accurately.**

## Editing your work

You can use a checklist like the one opposite to edit your work. Complete the checklist after each draft of a practice media text analysis. Aim to tick every cell of the final column.

 

| What you should check | First draft | Second draft | Third draft |
|---|---|---|---|
| **Analysis** | | | |
| You have correctly identified the key details of the text, including the writer, the purpose, the title, the text type, the place of publication, the intended audience and the main contention. | | | |
| You have included at least one quotation from the text in every paragraph. | | | |
| Every example is linked to its intended effect on the audience. | | | |
| The analysis considers how the argument and language have been shaped for the specific audience/s of the text. | | | |
| A paragraph or several sentences have been devoted to analysing the visual, audio or audiovisual material. | | | |
| **Language** | | | |
| Quotations from the text are accurate. | | | |
| Vocabulary and sentence structures are varied. | | | |
| Grammar, punctuation and spelling are correct. | | | |

EDIT

1 **Work with a practice analysis you have previously completed. Read your work to identify and amend:**

- **any spelling, punctuation or grammatical errors**
- **any examples for which an intended effect isn't identified**
- **any incorrect quotations from the text**
- **at least two repeated words or phrases that could be replaced with synonyms**
- **one overly long sentence that could be replaced with a simpler one.**

**2 Swap analyses with a partner and complete the following tasks.**

- **Identify two strengths of your partner's analysis.**
- **Identify two ways in which your partner's analysis could be improved. Give specific suggestions for achieving this.**

## Common mistakes and tips for top responses

The table below outlines some common mistakes made in media text analyses and explains how to fix them.

| Common mistakes | Solutions |
|---|---|
| Summarising the argument or content of the text | You are not required to explain the viewpoint presented but instead should analyse *how* the writer conveys it. Check that each statement you have made about a text comments on the writer's intended effect on the reader. |
| Expressing a personal view on the issue | None of your statements should suggest, either explicitly or implicitly, that you endorse or disagree with an opinion expressed in the text. Avoid the first-person 'I' in your analysis. |
| Making general statements and using vague expressions | Use strong, precise verbs and adjectives to analyse specific examples of language use. Think about the connotations of words and the exact emotions the writer is aiming to evoke. |
| Evaluating the effectiveness of the text's argument and language | Focus on the *intended* effect on the target audience; do not make judgements as to whether this is achieved. Avoid terms like 'effective' and 'successfully'. Replace phrases like 'makes the audience feel' with 'aims to make the audience feel'. |

Keep in mind the following advice for producing a high-level media text analysis.

- **Quote frequently from the text** but avoid long quotations as these take up valuable space that should be used to present your own analysis.
- **Include analyses of word choices**, considering their connotations and intended effects on the audience.
- **Consider all visual, audio or audiovisual material**, including elements such as borders, fonts, banners, speakers, tone of voice, music and so on.
- **Reflect on the specific audience and context**. Read any background information carefully and refer to it in your analysis.

 

Chapter 04

## UNIT 4 OUTCOME 2 (TASK 2):

# Points of view on issues

For Unit 4 Outcome 2 Task 2, you must present, in oral form, a point of view on an issue, using well-reasoned arguments and persuasive language. The point of view needs to relate to an issue that has appeared in the media since 1 September of the previous year. The issue does not have to be the same one that you studied for Unit 4 Outcome 2 Task 1.

The oral presentation is worth 20 marks. Your school will confirm the required length of your presentation; a typical length is three to five minutes.

## What you need to know

This section summarises everything you need to know to successfully complete this SAC task.

### Performance descriptors

Your presentation will be assessed against a set of performance descriptors. The 'very high' performance descriptors – which describe a response likely to receive between 17 and 20 marks out of a maximum of 20 – are reproduced in the left-hand column in the following table. The right-hand column presents advice on how to achieve this.

| 'Very high' performance descriptors | What you need to do |
|---|---|
| Creates a contention that addresses the complexity of the issue and composes an engaging presentation to position the intended audience, employing a complex set of sequenced arguments linked clearly to the contention. | Ensure your contention is clear, practical and relevant. You should be able to summarise it in a single sentence. |
| | Support your contention with at least three reasons. |
| | Organise your argument logically, so that your reasons are easily identifiable and their connection to your contention is clear. |

| 'Very high' performance descriptors | What you need to do |
|---|---|
| Integrates relevant and compelling evidence into all supporting arguments with a clear intention to create a persuasive effect. | Use relevant evidence to support each of your reasons. |
| | Present a variety of evidence, including facts, statistics and expert testimony. |
| | Use reliable evidence from credible sources. Facts and figures should be current. |
| Employs appropriate and persuasive vocabulary, including the use of specialist language, and creative language features to create a presentation that positions the audience. | Decide exactly what you want your audience to think and to feel, so you can make language choices with these intended responses in mind. |
| | Draw on all you have learned about language techniques and connotated language to select words likely to have the intended emotional impact on your audience. |
| Creates an apt, sustained and individual voice connected appropriately with a clear context. | Tailor your arguments and language to your purpose, audience and the context in which you are delivering your message. |
| | Speak authentically, in a way that feels natural and comfortable to you (while also using appropriately persuasive language and a standard or formal register). |
| Uses structures and features seamlessly to create a spoken point of view text that position the audience in nuanced and subtle ways. | Use signposting (e.g. 'firstly', 'additionally', 'in summary') to help the audience follow the logical development of your argument. |
| | Keep your paragraphs and sentences concise so that your audience can easily understand them. |
| | Use paralinguistic strategies (e.g. pace, emphasis, pauses) to position your audience to respond favourably. |
| | Use body language and eye contact to support your delivery and strengthen your persuasive impact. |

## Key knowledge and skills

The key to success in this SAC task is having a clear *contention* presented through logical, distinct *reasons* (or arguments) supported by sound *evidence*. Think of your argument like a house: it requires a strong foundation (contention) and solid walls (reasons) held together with mortar (evidence). The appeal of the house is in its presentation, or facade: this is your choice of persuasive strategies to engage and persuade your audience.

 

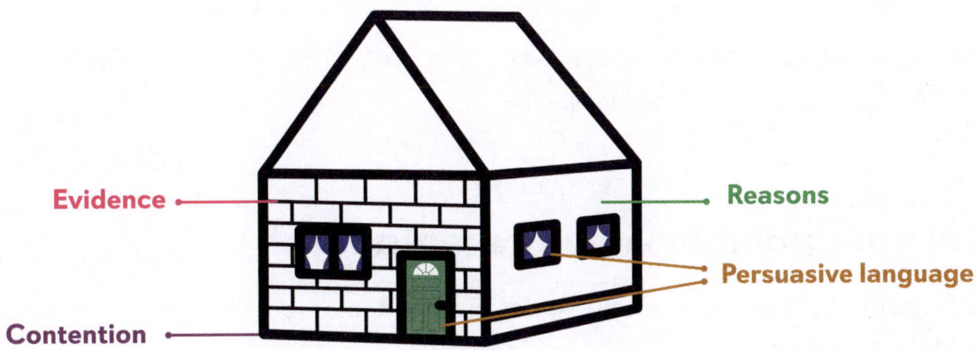


See also Chapter 3, which summarises the key concepts you will need to be familiar with to craft a well-reasoned, persuasively presented oral text.

MAP

**Using a draft or practice persuasive text you have written, create a diagram of a house like the one above, replacing the labels with the specific details of your text.**

# What you need to do

This section summarises everything you need to do to complete this SAC task.

## Prepare for the SAC task

In addition to the work you do in class for Unit 4 Outcome 2 Task 2, you can also prepare by following the suggestions below.

- **Read, listen to and watch a variety of media texts** on contemporary issues.
- **Keep a list of issues** that interest you and/or that you have a strong opinion about.
- **Pay attention to how other people present and support their opinions** on issues. Make notes on some of the common persuasive techniques you notice, especially those you think are particularly effective.
- **Notice how persuasive speakers engage their audiences** and try to shape their audiences' opinions. Make notes on the features particular to oral presentations.
- **Take opportunities to speak publicly.** Some ways you can do this before your SAC task include answering questions in class and rehearsing your point-of-view speech in front of family and friends.

Many, if not most, people feel nervous about having to present to an audience. The best way to tackle a fear of public speaking is to practise!

## Plan your point-of-view presentation

The first step is to choose an appropriate issue. Remember that your teacher will need to approve your choice. The issue must:

- have appeared in the media since 1 September of the previous year
- be one you can find plenty of information about
- provoke different points of view and discussion.

Once you have chosen your issue, you need to gather information on it. Sources you could look at include:

- online news sources and print newspapers
- websites and blogs
- streaming media (e.g. television documentaries, videos, podcasts).

You should gather information from a variety of sources representing a range of viewpoints. One way to keep track of your research is to create a summary sheet like the one below.

| Sources | Source titles and authors | Viewpoints | Reasons | Your responses |
|---|---|---|---|---|
| *The Conversation* | 'Pokies line the coffers of governments and venues – but there are ways to tame this gambling gorilla' by Charles Livingstone | The Australian Government should introduce measures to curb people's spending on poker machines. | Pokies are prevalent and addictive.<br>Users are manipulated and disadvantaged by the ways in which poker machines function.<br>Pre-commitment spending limits and banning gambling ads would help reduce problematic gambling behaviour. | Strongly agree. Pokies are highly addictive, leading to problem gambling. Measures to reduce the social harm they cause should be taken. |

 

The next step is to decide your own point of view on the issue. Try to express your viewpoint in a single sentence, using this stem: 'I believe that ...'

Your point of view summarised in a sentence is your *contention*, which you will support using several main *reasons*: these will form the 'walls' of your argument. Complete the sentence stem below by adding the main reasons for your contention.

I believe that [contention] ... because [reason 1] ____________

____________ [reason 2] ____________

____________ [reason 3] ____________

[reason 4] ____________

The following planning template will help you to select and organise your ideas before writing.

| Sections | What you should do |
|---|---|
| **Introduction** | Introduce the issue. |
| | Clearly state your main contention. |
| | Give an overview of your main supporting reasons. |
| **Body paragraphs** | Include a few short body paragraphs. |
| | Present one main reason and supporting evidence in each body paragraph. |
| | Structure each body paragraph around a topic sentence (usually the first sentence) expressing the main idea for that paragraph, followed by an explanation of the reason and/or evidence. |
| | At least one paragraph should include a rebuttal of the opposing viewpoints. |
| **Conclusion** | Reiterate your contention. |
| | Summarise your reasons. |
| | End with a call to action, direct appeal to the audience or memorable quotation to leave a strong impression with your audience. |

A rebuttal of opposing viewpoints can be incorporated into your body paragraphs or summarised in a single paragraph. If you take the second approach, your rebuttal should be presented in the paragraph just before your conclusion.

# Writing a point of view on an issue

This section contains advice, guidelines and word banks for writing your point of view on an issue. Remember that you will likely be expected to speak for between three and five minutes. This means that you should write between 600 and 800 words, depending on your pace (how slowly or quickly you speak).

## Elements of point-of-view presentations

Key elements of point-of-view presentations include the following.

### Introduction

The introduction is your first opportunity to make a strong persuasive impression on your audience. Here are some effective opening tactics.

- **Relate the topic to your audience.** You might identify a way in which the issue affects their everyday lives.
- **Ask the audience a question.** You could ask, 'How many of you have experienced ...?' or 'Can I get a show of hands from everyone who has heard of ...?'
- **Present a relevant and compelling statistic.** You might state the number of people or the percentage of the population affected by your chosen issue.
- **Tell an anecdote.** You could describe a situation in which the issue affected you or someone you know to illustrate its real-world impact.

Next, introduce the issue and provide some background information about it. Briefly explain how it developed and identify some of the main stakeholders and their viewpoints.

You should also state a *clear, strong contention* in the first few sentences, along with an *overview of the main reasons* for your point of view.

You can use the following sentence starters in your introduction.

| Introduction sentence starters |
|---|
| Have you ever stopped to consider ...? |
| How many of you here have experienced/felt/wondered ...? |
| An interesting thing happened to me the other day ... |
| Did you know that ...? |
| You might be surprised to learn that ... |
| [Well-known person] put it well when they said ... |

 

## Body paragraphs

Each body paragraph should focus on a reason for your contention and should include appropriate evidence. The following tips will help you to write strong body paragraphs.

- **Choose emotive words with care** to match the style and tone of your writing. While well-chosen emotive terms can be persuasive, frequent use of highly emotive language can undermine a logical argument. Develop your vocabulary so that you can use degrees of emotiveness consciously and effectively.
- **Think about how those on the opposing side of the debate could attack your points** and how you would counter these attacks to make your case convincing.
- **Stay on message**. Always keep in mind your purpose and main contention. You don't need to include every piece of information or idea your research has uncovered. Instead, you should be selective, including only details and reasons that best support your arguments.
- **Write for the ear**. Remember that you are writing a speech, not an essay. People will be listening to your words rather than reading them. Avoid very long or complex sentences, include pauses so the audience can absorb important points, and use techniques like directly addressing the audience members to hold their attention.
- **Use numerical markers** to help your audience follow the argument (e.g. 'the first point … the second point …').
- **Use visual material**, if appropriate (e.g. a slide show including graphs, charts and images). Remember that any visual material you present should *support*, not distract from, your presentation.

Note that none of the performance descriptors on pages 69–70 specifically mention visual material. So don't spend much time preparing elaborate slide shows; your focus should be on the content and delivery of your speech.

You can use the following sentence starters in your body paragraphs.

| Body paragraph sentence starters |
|---|
| I'd like to begin by … |
| Firstly, … Secondly, … |
| According to [expert], … |

| Body paragraph sentence starters |
| --- |
| As reported in [publication], … |
| The evidence demonstrates that … |

## Conclusion

The conclusion should strongly reiterate your contention and present a summary of your reasons. It should leave your audience with a persuasive final impression. Effective ways to finish your speech include:

- **a call to action** (e.g. asking your audience to stop eating certain products, to write to their local member of parliament or to sign a petition)
- **a rhetorical question** (e.g. 'Wouldn't the world be a better place if …?' or 'Isn't it about time that …?')
- **an inspiring quotation** (e.g. a statement by a well-known figure who has encapsulated a 'big idea' connected to your chosen issue).

You can use the following sentence starters in your conclusion.

| Conclusion sentence starters |
| --- |
| I hope that we can all agree … |
| Having outlined the reasons for [your opinion], I trust that I can count on you all to [desired response]. |
| In summary, it is clear that … |
| As we have seen, there can be no doubt that … |
| In the words of [well-known person], … |
| Let's all work together to … |

WRITE

**Choose a sentence starter from each of the introduction, body paragraph and conclusion sentence starter tables on pages 74–6 and write three complete sentences about an issue and contention of your choice.**

 

## Improve and rehearse your point-of-view presentation

You will have the opportunity to draft and rehearse your point-of-view presentation before you deliver it for your SAC task. The following advice could help you to improve your presentation from a 'medium' to a 'very high' performance.

### Understanding the issue

You must show that you understand the issue. Here are some tips.

- **Provide details about the issue** (e.g. what the main points of view are, how it affects people, how the debate arose, why you feel it is important).
- **Select evidence carefully**, making sure it is significant and relevant to the reason it is supporting. If you have thoroughly researched your issue, you should have much more information than you can include, so choose the most effective evidence.
- **Use evidence from reputable sources** (e.g. information on a government website is likely to be more reliable than information on a personal blog).
- **Be specific about the sources** of your information. If you refer to expert testimony, specify the expert's name and position and explain the relevance of their experience and expertise. If you present statistics, say where you found them.

### Presenting your reasons

Make sure your audience understands your reasons. Here are some tips.

- **Pay attention to the structure of your presentation.** Order your reasons carefully to create the most persuasive impact on your audience.
- **Use logical language** (e.g. 'therefore', 'in consequence') to present a coherent argument and to show how the evidence supports your reasons.
- **Use transition words** between paragraphs (points of argument), so that your points flow smoothly and logically.

### Features of persuasive oral presentations

Use the features of an oral presentation to maximise your persuasive effect. Here are some tips.

- **Use appropriate persuasive language**, drawing on your knowledge of persuasive writing and speaking.
- **Use strategies and techniques appropriate to the oral medium** (e.g. body language and gestures, variation in the pitch and volume of your voice) to evoke targeted reactions in the audience.

## Editing your work

You can use a checklist like the one below to edit your work. Complete the checklist after each draft of a point-of-view text. Aim to tick every cell of the final column.

| What you should check | First draft | Second draft | Third draft |
|---|---|---|---|
| **Structure** | | | |
| The introduction engages the audience and clearly presents the speaker's point of view on the issue. | | | |
| Each body paragraph includes a topic sentence identifying the focus of the paragraph. | | | |
| Each body paragraph develops a supporting reason. | | | |
| The conclusion summarises the argument and leaves the audience with a strong impression. | | | |
| **Argument** | | | |
| The point of view is supported by three or four separate strong reasons. | | | |
| Each reason is supported by relevant evidence. | | | |
| Evidence is drawn from a variety of credible and authoritative sources. | | | |
| Media sources and references are appropriately cited. | | | |
| **Language** | | | |
| The text includes persuasive words and phrases to create particular effects on the audience. | | | |
| Strategies employed are appropriate for an oral presentation and aimed at engaging a listening audience. | | | |
| Paragraphs are linked by appropriate connecting words. | | | |
| The lengths and structures of sentences are varied. | | | |

Swap the text of your presentation with a partner and, after reading each other's text, complete the following questions or tasks.

1 Can you identify the contention? Is it clearly expressed?

2 Are the reasons underpinning the point of view clear and supported by relevant evidence?

3 Identify five examples of persuasive language in the piece.

4 Is the piece suited to an oral presentation? Does it engage the audience with some direct address? Is there clear signposting of the main reasons?

5 Write down three suggestions for improving your partner's piece.

6 Exchange feedback and edit your pieces according to each other's comments.

## Practising your point-of-view presentation

You should practise reading your speech aloud multiple times before you present it. The more thoroughly you know your speech, the more confident you will feel when presenting it, and the less reliant you will be on your written notes.

The first time you practise, focus on identifying issues that you can fix by redrafting your speech. Carry out the following checks.

**Your speech should be an appropriate length.** Remember that you're likely to speak faster when you're doing your actual presentation, so make sure you have enough content to fill the required time.

If your speech is too long, check for repetition or points of minor importance that could be omitted. If it's too short, look for reasons that could be explained in more detail or supported by further evidence. Alternatively, you might need to do some more research to find another strong reason for your opinion.

**Avoid very long sentences.** They can be hard to say without pausing for breath. Identify long sentences that you can break up into shorter sentences.

**Find a pronunciation guide online.** You can use it if you are unsure how to pronounce particular words. Check also for words or names in your speech that are difficult to say and practise them repeatedly until you feel confident.

**Include pauses in appropriate places.** These allow time for the audience to absorb important points and ensure you aren't rushing through your speech. During pauses, make eye contact with the audience.

**Use body language to influence and engage your audience.** Consider where you could point to the audience, raise an arm, nod or shake your head and so on.

REHEARSE

**Prepare a speech on an issue that you feel strongly about. Then, working with a partner and a speech they have prepared, complete the following tasks.**

1 **Deliver your speeches while you record each other on your phones.**

2 **Watch the speeches together and prepare notes using the checklist below.**

**The speaker:**

- ☐ **established sufficient eye contact with the audience**
- ☐ **maintained a natural speaking pace: neither too fast nor too slow**
- ☐ **paused after making an important point**
- ☐ **spoke at an appropriate volume**
- ☐ **spoke clearly, without mumbling**
- ☐ **kept a relaxed stance and used gestures where appropriate**
- ☐ **spoke for an appropriate length of time**
- ☐ **used relevant and informative visual material (if any) that did not distract from the speech.**

3 **Deliver your speeches again, taking the notes in your checklists into account.**

## Present your point of view

This section contains advice for using cue cards and delivering an effective oral presentation.

### Using cue cards

You need to know your speech well and practise it repeatedly. Cue cards should be used as a memory aid only. The following tips will help you to use cue cards effectively.

- **Do not write your whole speech on cue cards.** If you do, you will end up with too many to handle, the writing will be too cramped to read, and you will spend your time peering at cards rather than engaging with your audience.
- **Use cue cards that fit into the palm of your hand.** Write your notes in large, clear letters and colour-code them (e.g. highlight main points in green and quotations in blue).
- **Write one main point on each card.** Use bullet points for evidence, capital letters for examples and lower-case letters for quotations. Use only abbreviations you recognise.

 

- **Number your cards** and write on one side only.
- **Write 'PAUSE' where necessary** to remind you to stop at important points.

### Delivering your oral presentation

The advice below will help you to present your point of view confidently and effectively.

- **Slow down.** It's natural to speak more quickly when you're nervous, so make a conscious effort to regulate the pace of your speaking. Aim to speak at aound 120 to 130 words per minute, so your audience can easily comprehend your argument. This is a slower speed than you would use when talking with friends.
- **Vary your pace and volume.** This will help you to emphasise key points and add interest to the listening experience for your audience.
- **Make eye contact.** This is essential for engaging your audience. Make eye contact with various individuals. Don't stare at one person or a spot on the wall, or some audience members will feel excluded. If you get nervous, look just above everyone's heads, and you will appear to be interacting with the audience.
- **Breathe.** It sounds simple, but remembering to take deep breaths between the transitions in your speech will help to slow your pace and make you appear more comfortable in front of the audience.
- **Don't panic.** If you lose your place or get flustered, pause and give yourself a moment to calm down. Briefly apologise to your audience, locate your place on your cue cards and repeat, in your mind, the last sentence you said aloud. This should jog your memory of where you were up to.

## Common mistakes and tips for top responses

The following table outlines some common mistakes made in point-of-view presentations and explains how to fix them.

| Common mistakes | Solutions |
|---|---|
| Not supporting the opinion with logically ordered reasons | Make a list of the reasons you are using to support your point of view. You should have at least three separate strong reasons. Identify where you have articulated these in your piece. If you can't easily do this, it is likely you haven't satisfactorily backed up your opinion.<br>Try expressing each reason as a statement that can become the topic sentence of a body paragraph. |

| Common mistakes | Solutions |
|---|---|
| Not supporting reasons with evidence | You must provide facts, statistics, expert testimony and so on to substantiate your reasons. Read over your work and highlight every piece of evidence you have included. If any reasons are not supported by evidence or are supported by inadequate evidence, you might need to do some more research to find suitable information. |
| Being informative rather than persuasive | Your speech should include the sorts of language and strategies suited to a persuasive oral text. Try directly addressing the audience, asking rhetorical questions and using inclusive language to engage your audience. |
| Giving a dull presentation | You need to vary the pace, volume and tone of your voice and to use effective body language. Practise in front of the mirror and/or record yourself presenting your speech. Analyse your performance critically or ask a friend for feedback. You can also use tools such as Microsoft's PowerPoint, which can give you feedback about aspects of your delivery. How could you use facial expressions, body language and eye contact more effectively? |

Keep in mind the following advice for producing a high-level point-of-view presentation on an issue.

- **Have a clear structure.** This is especially important for an oral text. The audience needs to be able to understand the issue and follow your reasoning straight away; they cannot go back over anything they don't immediately grasp. Always keep the audience's needs in mind.
- **Make the most of the medium.** Take the opportunity to use your voice, facial expressions and body language to persuade the audience.
- **Draw on your study of persuasive texts.** Having analysed persuasive texts, you should have a solid understanding of common persuasive strategies. Make sure you use them in your own persuasive text.

 

# Chapter 05

# The exam

The end-of-Year-12 English exam contributes 50 per cent of your study score. It has a duration of three hours, with an additional 15 minutes of reading time. It is divided into three equally weighted sections, each worth one-third of the exam score.

| Task | You must write | What you should do |
|---|---|---|
| **Section A** | | |
| Analytical response to a text | ONE analytical essay on ONE text | Demonstrate your knowledge of the text, your ability to write an analytical essay and your use of evidence to support an argument. |
| **Section B** | | |
| Creating a text | ONE piece of original writing | Draw on ideas from the Framework you have been studying, use the title and stimulus material and create a text with a clear purpose and voice. |
| **Section C** | | |
| Analysis of argument and language | ONE analytical essay on a persuasive text | Understand arguments, analyse written language and visuals, and use evidence to support your analysis. |

You should be familiar with the assessment criteria and performance descriptors, which you can find on the VCAA website: https://www.vcaa.vic.edu.au/assessment/vce/examination-specifications-past-examinations-and-examination-reports/english

## General study tips

The advice below will help you prepare in the weeks leading up to your exam period.

**Create a study schedule.** You will likely have exams for your other subjects, too. In the weeks leading up to your exams, allocate time to study for each subject.

**Practise handwriting.** You might not be used to writing by hand for an extended period. In the lead-up to the exam, handwrite as much as possible to improve your speed, legibility and stamina.

**Complete practice exams and sample tasks under exam conditions.** Some organisations produce trial exams or exam revision material specifically for Year 12 English. Your teacher might also be able to give you practice material for each section of the exam.

You could work with a partner or small study group to create and share topics on your text, titles and stimulus material, and persuasive texts for analysis.

**Proofread your practice pieces.** Get into the habit of reading every practice piece you write to check for spelling, grammar and punctuation errors, as well as for fluency and clarity of expression. You should also try swapping work with a partner and correcting each other's work.

The more you practise the skill of identifying and fixing errors, the better you will get at proofreading your work in a time-limited situation like an exam.

**Read past exam reports.** The exam reports on the VCAA website are written by senior VCAA English assessors. They offer advice on what assessors are looking for in exam responses and explain common mistakes that students make in each section of the exam.

## Incorporating teacher feedback

A key way to optimise your performance in the exam is to make a conscious effort to incorporate your teacher's feedback on previous work into your exam practice pieces. Try the following.

**Look over recent feedback.** Make sure you understand it. If anything is unclear to you, ask your teacher to explain it. Do you notice any patterns in the suggestions your teacher has given you in the previous year or so? Are there particular areas where you struggle or have scope for improvement?

**Make notes.** When your teacher gives you oral feedback, making written notes will help you to remember it.

**Draw a table.** Use a table like the one below to record previous feedback and to set goals, in consultation with your teacher.

| Feedback and goals | My opinion | My teacher's opinion |
|---|---|---|
| My strengths are | | |
| I need to work on | | |
| In my next practice piece, I will | | |

 

**Be systematic.** Tackle the suggestions from your teacher one at a time. It can be helpful to begin with the big-picture areas for improvement (e.g. a lack of textual evidence in a text-response essay) before tackling smaller details (e.g. incorrect punctuation).

**Practise self-assessment.** Before or just after submitting a piece of writing, try predicting what your teacher's comments will be. Make notes, then see how close your predictions were. If they were very different from your teacher's thoughts, you might need to check your understanding of the qualities of a high-level response with your teacher.

DEVELOP

1 **Revisit feedback from your teacher on your previous assessment submissions and practice pieces.**

2 **Identify areas to target for growth (e.g. quality of ideas, use of metalanguage, sequencing of arguments, adherence to the topic).**

3 **Create practice paragraphs or complete pieces that home in on these areas.**

4 **Submit these for feedback to see if you have developed your skills.**

## Managing your time in the exam

You have 15 minutes of reading time and three hours of writing time. During the reading time, you may not write anything; however, you may check the meanings of words in your dictionary.

Use the reading time to:

- select your topic for Section A
- consider the Section B title and stimuli for your Framework
- read the Section C resource material – this should take up the bulk of your reading time.

Allocate one hour of writing time to each of the three sections. For Sections A and B, brainstorm and plan carefully before writing each piece. For Section C, instead of writing a plan, spend time annotating the text.

Pay full attention to every word on the exam paper and follow every instruction. Use a black pen to write your answers.

You may choose the order in which you complete the tasks. However, consider completing Section C first, because, as previously noted, you should spend most of the reading time on this section, and it will be fresh in your mind.

A possible way to manage your time in the exam is shown below.

| What you need to do | Minutes allocated | |
|---|---|---|
| **Section A** | | |
| Planning: interpret the question, brainstorm, group ideas into points, formulate point of view or contention, map out main points (draft topic sentences) | 6 | 60 minutes |
| Introduction | 3 | |
| Body paragraphs | 45 | |
| Conclusion | 3 | |
| Proofreading | 3 | |
| **Section B** | | |
| Planning: determine which stimulus/stimuli to use, brainstorm, group ideas into points, formulate point of view or contention, map out main points, determine audience, decide purpose and genre | 6 | 60 minutes |
| Introduction | 3 | |
| Body paragraphs | 45 | |
| Conclusion | 3 | |
| Proofreading | 3 | |
| **Section C** | | |
| Second reading (first reading completed during reading time): begin to annotate | 4 | 60 minutes |
| Third reading: complete annotation | 3 | |
| Introduction | 3 | |
| Body paragraphs | 45 | |
| Conclusion | 2 | |
| Proofreading | 3 | |

Some troubleshooting tips are provided below.

- If you make a mistake, rule a line through the word and write above it. Do not use liquid paper.
- If you start in the wrong section of the answer book, call the supervisor.
- If you leave something out, write the missing text at the end of the section and put an asterisk and the words 'see information at end' where the missing text should have been.
- If you are running out of time to complete a section, write your remaining responses in dot-point form and then write the conclusion.

# Section A: Analytical response to a text

For this section of the exam, you have to write an analytical essay in response to one of two topics on your set text. Remember that a well-written, concise response will gain more marks than a poorly written, largely irrelevant but longer response.

## Assessment criteria

Your essay will be assessed according to the criteria reproduced in the left-hand column in the table below. The right-hand column presents advice on how to address this criteria.

| Criteria | What you need to do |
|---|---|
| Knowledge and understanding of the text, its structure, and the ideas, concerns and values it explores | Know and understand the text thoroughly. You should have read or viewed it multiple times before the exam. |
| | Develop a clear contention in response to the topic. |
| | Select appropriate textual evidence to support your contention. |
| Development of a coherent analysis in response to the topic | Apply the principles of essay writing, with a clear introduction; body paragraphs that develop a logical, well-supported interpretation; and a conclusion. |
| | Respond to all parts of the topic. |
| Use of evidence from the text to support the analysis | Support your response with examples, quotations and references to structural features that are both accurate and relevant. |
| Use of fluent expression through appropriate use of vocabulary and conventions of Standard Australian English | Use appropriate metalanguage for analysing texts, including your specific text type. |
| | Use a variety of sentence structures. |
| | Demonstrate accurate grammar, spelling and punctuation. |

In addition to the assessment criteria listed on the previous page, your work will be assessed using the 'Expected qualities for the mark range – Section A', which can be found on the VCAA website: https://www.vcaa.vic.edu.au/assessment/vce/examination-specifications-past-examinations-and-examination-reports/english

The qualities necessary for essays to be scored in the top three mark ranges are reproduced below. The distinguishing qualities of a Section A analytical response worth nine to ten marks are highlighted.

| Marks | Expected qualities |
|---|---|
| 9–10 | Demonstrates a close and perceptive reading of the text, considering complexities of its ideas, concerns and values explored through the structure of the text and its language |
| | Demonstrates a clear understanding of the implications of the topic, using an appropriate strategy for dealing with it, and exploring its complexity from the basis of the text |
| | Develops a cogent, controlled and well-substantiated discussion using precise and expressive language |
| 8 | Demonstrates a thoughtful reading of the text, exploring its ideas, concerns and values through a discussion of the structure of the text and its language |
| | Demonstrates an understanding of the implications of the topic, exploring it from the basis of the text |
| | Develops a detailed, substantiated and coherent discussion using language fluently and confidently |
| 7 | Demonstrates detailed knowledge of the text throughout, including some of its ideas, concerns and values by appropriately acknowledging aspects of the structure of the text and its language |
| | Understands the topic, developing a sustained and well-supported response |
| | Develops an organised piece of writing using language accurately and appropriately |

## Features of high-, medium- and low-range responses

Previous exam reports have noted the following features of *high-range essays*.

- They show a thorough understanding of the task requirements and a deep and broad knowledge of the text, which can allow the student to use this to challenge the idea in the topic (where appropriate).

 

- The introductions articulate a clear response to the essay topic.
- They contain relevant discussion of specific textual features, including structural elements.
- They stay focused on the topic throughout.
- Fluency of language and a wide vocabulary allow the students to express thoughtful and complex ideas.

Previous exam reports have noted the following features of *medium- to low-range essays*.

- They display knowledge and understanding of the text; however, this is not linked sufficiently to the topic.
- They address only part of the topic.
- They lapse into storytelling, which can demonstrate a student's knowledge of the plot but not much else.
- A lack of vocabulary limits the exploration of ideas.
- They are poorly structured and organised.
- They may show token attempts at relevance by including key words from the topic; however, they do not clearly and consistently address the topic.

## Preparing for Section A

The most important aspect of your revision is re-reading or re-watching your text and making sure you know it thoroughly. You should have a strong understanding of the ideas, concerns and values the text's creator is exploring and the messages they aim to communicate.

The following strategies will help you revise your text and prepare for writing an analytical text response.

**Create a file of notes on your text.** You might divide these into categories (e.g. information and ideas about characters, about concerns and values, and so on).

**Memorise key spellings and textual details.** You should know how to spell the title of your text and the name of the writer or director, as well as the names of the characters and places in the text.

Writing down these key details multiple times, by hand, will help you to remember them and will also provide valuable handwriting practice. Place sticky notes around your desk with author, character and place names written on them, so you see them frequently.

**Develop quotation banks.** Try to memorise approximately 20 key quotations. These don't have to be long: each should be under ten words, and some might be just a key word or phrase. Choose a range of quotations that say something significant about major concepts or tensions in the text, or reveal important aspects of main characters and their relationships.

You might write out each quotation in black and notes about the context (who said it, to whom, when, under what circumstances) in blue. You could write these on sticky notes as well, to help cement them in your mind.

**Summarise the plot.** Make sure you know the essential details of your text: what happens when, where and to whom. Summarise the events in a time line, flowchart or table. It can also be helpful to explain the plot to a friend or family member, to check your recollection of important events.

**Understand the context and background of your text.** Being aware of relevant background information about your text is especially important if it is set in an historical period or an unfamiliar setting (e.g. to really understand Sarah Moss' *Ghost Wall* you should understand something about social and geographical divisions in contemporary England). Try summarising relevant background information in dot-point form or explaining it to a friend to solidify your understanding.

**Create interpretive statements.** The topics in this section of the exam will focus on the ideas, concerns and values – or big ideas – in the text. Make a list of three or four of these key ideas, then write an interpretive statement about each (e.g. if you identified 'courage' as a major idea in your text, your interpretive statement might say 'The author suggests that sometimes it takes more courage to refrain from acting than it does to take action'. Next, find three key quotations or other pieces of textual evidence to support each interpretive statement.

**Generate word banks for the text's big ideas and concerns.** Be alert to nuances in the meanings of the different words and practise using them to extend and develop your interpretative statements and your understanding of the big ideas.

**Identify some of the text creator's strategies for creating meaning.** These might include motif, setting, imagery, narrative voice, camera angle and editing. Practise incorporating these into your paragraphs so that you demonstrate awareness of how these elements build meaning.

**Write essay topics and plans.** Creating your own topics makes you think carefully about the text and about the importance of each word in a topic. You can then swap topics with a partner and practise writing plans and essays in response to new topics.

 

**Obtain sample essays and try marking them yourself.** Use the assessment criteria and comment on how the essays could be improved.

**Read other students' assessed essays.** Pay attention to the assessor's comments, noting how you could apply their advice to your own work.

*Do not* rote-learn essays. It only takes a single word change to alter a topic significantly. You have not previously responded to the topic you choose in the exam, unless it is exactly the same, *word for word*!

PLAN

1. **Develop five topics on your text, using the examples in this book or those given to you in class as models.**
2. **Create an essay plan for each topic. Give yourself ten minutes to:**
   - **brainstorm relevant ideas and group ideas that connect**
   - **articulate a contention**
   - **create a topic sentence for each body paragraph**
   - **make dot-point notes about relevant textual evidence**
   - **make notes on what the evidence reveals about a particular idea.**
3. **Drawing on your notes from question 2, write an introductory paragraph for each essay.**

## Completing Section A

Choose your topic during the reading time. During the writing time, read the topic again carefully to make sure you understand exactly what it is asking you to do. Identify the key terms, so you are clear about your focus.

The most critical mistakes are often made in the first five minutes, when students are determining what the question they have chosen is asking, brainstorming, writing a plan and drafting a contention and topic sentences. Pay close attention to every word in the topic.

Next, form a contention in response to the topic. Spend a few minutes writing a brief plan that includes your contention, three or four topic sentences, and one or two pieces of textual evidence for each topic sentence.

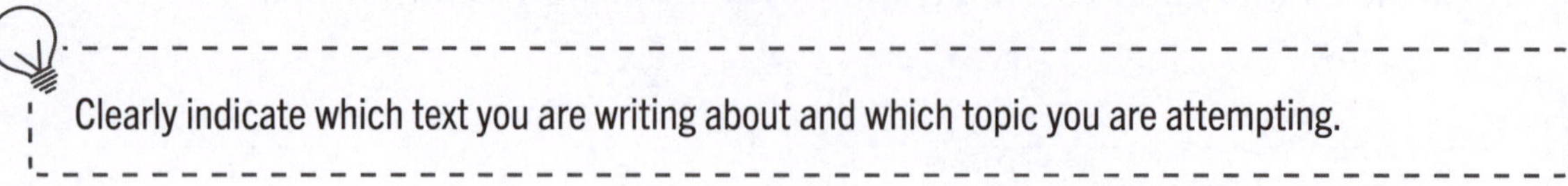

Clearly indicate which text you are writing about and which topic you are attempting.

The following advice will help you to write an effective analytical text response in an exam.

## Responding to the topic

Respond to the complete topic. Weaker text responses often focus just on one main idea in a topic. Stronger responses address every word in the topic, including limiting words (such as 'always' and 'never').

Many topics require you to agree or disagree with a statement. Partially agreeing can often lead to a more sophisticated and thoughtful response that shows you have thought deeply about the complexities of the text.

In addition, clearly articulate what you think the writer is aiming to communicate, in relation to the topic. In your body paragraphs, explain *how* they are doing this.

Exam reports often note that while many students write a response that shows good knowledge of the text, the response is only marginally relevant to the topic.

## Structuring your essay

Establish your contention or interpretation clearly in your introduction. Organise your body paragraphs around ideas or concerns. Most topics will ask you to explore the text's big ideas rather than individual characters. When you do discuss characters, link them to the larger messages of the text.

Use the conclusion to reaffirm your argument and resolve the topic. Consider what the text or writer reveals about human nature or human behaviour in relation to the topic. If possible, articulate what the purpose of that revelation might be; for example, the text might reveal that the natural world is affected by human action, and the writer's purpose might be to exhort readers to treat the natural world with respect.

 

### Using evidence

To support your argument, refer to a variety of textual features, not just characters or events in the plot. For example, consider the structure of the text, the setting/s and the use of symbols. Refer to film techniques if you are analysing a film and to stage directions if you are writing about a play. Using a variety of textual evidence shows that you know your text very well and helps you to present a deeper, more thoughtful response.

Your essay should include quotations from the text, but they shouldn't be scattered haphazardly throughout. Choose quotations carefully to support the points you are making and integrate them smoothly into your sentences. Avoid using quotations as standalone sentences and starting or ending paragraphs with a quotation. Instead, weave short quotations into your sentences and explain why they are significant and how they support your point.

Metalanguage allows you to communicate your ideas clearly and precisely. Strong text responses use metalanguage specific to the type of text being discussed. If you are studying a film, use terms like 'cross-cut' and 'mise en scène'; if you are studying a collection of poems, refer to 'rhythm' and 'stanzas'. You should be able to discuss how and why techniques generate meaning in the text.

## Section B: Creating a text

For this section of the exam, you have to write one text in a form of your choosing (not including song, poetry or verse). In your text, you must include meaningful connections with ideas drawn from:

- one of the Frameworks of Ideas
- the title provided for your selected Framework of Ideas
- at least one piece of stimulus material for your selected Framework of Ideas.

The stimulus material is likely to consist of three items, such as:

- a quotation or statement
- an image
- a short poem or an extract from a poem.

You must develop your text with a clear purpose, incorporating at least one of the four main purposes of writing: to explain, to reflect, to express and to argue. You should write an effective and cohesive text that demonstrates fluency through your selection of structure, vocabulary and language features.

## Assessment criteria

Your text will be assessed according to the criteria reproduced in the left-hand column in the table below. The right-hand column presents advice on how to address this criteria.

| Criteria | What you need to do |
| --- | --- |
| Use of relevant idea(s) drawn from one Framework of Ideas, the title provided and at least one piece of stimulus material | Show a clear focus on the title. The title should encapsulate the central idea of and be the focus for your piece of writing. |
| | Explore ideas connected to the Framework, showing that you have thought about these in depth and offering your own perspective on them. |
| | Use the stimulus material thoughtfully, as a source of inspiration or to develop the main ideas in your piece connected to the title and Framework. |
| Creation of a cohesive text that connects to a clear purpose(s) and incorporates an appropriate voice | Before you start writing, decide your writing purpose. (You may have more than one.) |
| | Craft a clear and original voice that supports your purpose and considers your likely audience. |
| Use of suitable text structure(s) and language features to create a text | Before you start writing, decide what form you will write in. (You may write in a hybrid form.) The form should be suitable for your purpose. |
| | Show that you are familiar with the features associated with your chosen text type by using them to help achieve your purpose. |
| Use of fluent expression, including the appropriate use of vocabulary | Use a wide vocabulary. When reading over your work, change any repetitive or dull word choices to more precise and interesting ones. |
| | Vary your sentence lengths. |
| | Take time to read your work and correct any errors in grammar, spelling or punctuation. |

In addition to the assessment criteria listed above, your work will be assessed using the 'Expected qualities for the mark range – Section B', which can be found on the VCAA website: https://www.vcaa.vic.edu.au/assessment/vce/examination-specifications-past-examinations-and-examination-reports/english

 

The qualities necessary for texts to be scored in the top three mark ranges are reproduced on the next page. The distinguishing qualities of a Section B text worth nine to ten marks are highlighted.

| Marks | Expected qualities |
|---|---|
| 9–10 | Demonstrates insightful consideration of the ideas raised by the title and stimulus in connection with a Framework of Ideas |
| | Creates a cohesive text with an explicit purpose(s) and an appropriate voice |
| | Demonstrates sophisticated control of language and text structure(s), that makes rich use of vocabulary and language features |
| 8 | Demonstrates an astute exploration of the ideas raised by the title and stimulus in connection with a Framework of Ideas |
| | Creates a coherent text with an explicit purpose(s) and an appropriate voice |
| | Demonstrates confident control of language and text structure(s), that makes thoughtful use of vocabulary and language features |
| 7 | Demonstrates a detailed connection to the ideas raised by the title and stimulus related to a Framework of Ideas |
| | Creates a coordinated text with a clear purpose(s) and an appropriate voice |
| | Demonstrates sound control of language and text structure(s), that makes clear use of vocabulary and language features |

You only have to incorporate *one* of the three stimuli in your writing. While you are permitted to incorporate two or three, you may struggle to use more than one or two effectively.

## Features of high-, medium- and low-range responses

Previous exam reports have noted the following features of *high-range texts*.

- They engage closely with the title, demonstrating that their writers have thought about it in some depth and engaged with its ideas.
- They feature a sustained and original voice.
- They are well structured and use the features of the chosen text type.
- Their purpose is clear.
- They use a wide vocabulary that allows in-depth exploration of ideas and precise expression of these ideas.

Previous exam reports have noted the following features of *medium- to low-range texts*.

- They do not show clear engagement with the topic and its ideas.
- They do not incorporate at least one of the stimuli.
- They lack a clear purpose.
- They simply tell a story, and don't use it as a vehicle to explore and develop ideas.
- They do not show close engagement with and deep understanding of ideas connected to the Framework.

Do not rote-learn a text and write it out verbatim. Even if it is a fluent and effective piece of writing that explores relevant Framework ideas in depth, it will almost certainly not be relevant to the title or the stimuli and thus unlikely to achieve high marks.

REVISE

**1 Swap practice pieces with a partner and, after reading each other's text, answer the following questions.**

- **What do you think is the purpose of the piece?**
- **Does the text respond to the title and stimulus material?**
- **Does it engage with ideas relevant to the Framework?**
- **Is the writing clear?**
- **Does the text flow logically?**
- **Is the voice appropriate to the form, purpose and intended audience?**

**2 Revise your piece according to your partner's feedback.**

## Preparing for Section B

Your preparation for this task involves two main activities: reviewing course material and practising exam-style tasks.

Begin by re-reading your mentor texts and the notes you made on them. Your aim is to re-familiarise yourself with the writing strategies the mentor texts use. (Note, however, that you are not required to incorporate the mentor texts' strategies into your writing in the exam.) You should also return to notes you made about key ideas in your Framework and add any new insights you might have.

 

Spend time completing exam-style tasks: practise planning and writing an original text in response to a title and stimulus material in one hour.

Make sure you can confidently write in at least two forms and for at least two main purposes. If you enter the exam expecting to write in only one form (such as a speech) with one purpose (such as to argue), you may find that your ideas, preferred writing format and purpose are not the best fit for the title and stimulus material you are presented with.

The following strategies will also help you hone your writing skills and prepare for writing an original text.

**Return to the file you should have been developing** throughout the year on the Framework you are studying. Focus now on formulating your own original ideas connected to the big idea. Make notes about different ways in which you might explore these ideas in original pieces of writing. This will provide a good bank of ideas to draw on and develop when responding to the title and stimulus material in the exam.

**Consider how the Framework or aspects of it connect to your own knowledge and interests.** Explore these connections to help you produce authentic and nuanced texts.

**Do some research relevant to your Framework.** This will help you develop your knowledge and enhance your exploration of ideas and the detail of your writing. For instance, if you wish to write a memoir or an imaginative piece, you might find that knowing names of specific plants in a garden setting will help you to build a convincing portrayal of it. If you are writing a persuasive or expository piece about a particular event or historical period, you might need to do some research on it.

**Develop your vocabulary.** This section of the exam is all about your writing skills (as well as the quality of your ideas), so ensure you enter the exam well prepared with a wide and precise vocabulary. Expand your vocabulary by creating word banks and lists of new words with definitions. Make a point of using a variety of words and newly learned terms in your practice pieces. Reading widely is also an excellent way to improve your vocabulary, as well as to find more ideas to explore in your writing.

However, be careful! Using too many complex or unusual words can make your writing sound awkward and overwritten. Develop your vocabulary so that you can choose the most precise and appropriate word in every instance, not so you can dazzle your reader with all the complex words you know.

**Create or curate sets of titles and stimulus material.** These should include evocative titles that suggest a range of ideas, short poems or text extracts, quotations and interesting images. Swap these sets with a partner or in a small group, to practise responding to stimuli.

1 **Search online for a quotation or an image related to the Framework you are studying. Write out the quotation or paste the image at the top of a piece of paper.**

2 **Create a short title connected to your Framework and write it on the same page.**

3 **Give yourself five minutes to create the outline of a response. Identify:**

- **a way to use the title**
- **key ideas to explore**
- **connections between the ideas and the Framework**
- **a way to use the quotation or image**
- **the text type you will write in**
- **the purpose of your piece**
- **the intended audience of your piece.**

## Completing Section B

Read the title and stimulus material very carefully during the reading time. Choose the stimulus or stimuli that you think you can most effectively incorporate into your piece.

During the writing time, follow the steps below to plan your piece.

**1.** Brainstorm relevant ideas in response to the title and stimulus or stimuli.

**2.** Determine the form, audience and purpose of your piece.

**3.** Divide your ideas into paragraphs.

The following advice will help you to write an effective original text.

### Responding to the title, stimulus material and Framework

Treat the title as the central idea in your piece of writing. Remember that you do not have to agree with any idea encapsulated in the title; you may choose to challenge it. You may choose to treat the title and stimulus material either literally or metaphorically.

Responding to the title means engaging directly with the idea/s it suggests. Your piece should be shaped around the title and show that you have thought about it in some depth. The title could provide the main theme, a character arc, an important symbol or another key element of your writing. The connection between the title and the content of your piece should be clear to the person marking your work.

You should also respond to at least one stimulus. You could do this by using the stimulus as a key idea in your text (providing this clearly works with the title) by including or referring to it at a key point in your text to reveal an important idea (though you do not need to refer to it specifically) or by setting your piece in the world of the stimulus (this is especially effective when your chosen stimulus is an image).

Your piece should also show an in-depth engagement with, and exploration of, ideas connected to the Framework and indicate that you have reached some conclusions of your own.

Note that you must identify on your script book which Framework of Ideas you are responding to and which stimulus or stimuli you are incorporating into your piece of writing. You do not have to identify on your script book the audience, purpose or form of your piece.

## Writing for a purpose and an audience

Carefully consider your purpose and your target audience. It is advisable to choose an audience of people your age or older, as it is hard to produce a sophisticated and subtle text for a very young target audience. Your audience and purpose should be clear to your assessor from your choices about form, subject matter and language.

## Creating an effective and cohesive text

Your text must clearly employ the structural and stylistic features of the form you are writing in. Whatever type of text you produce, it should have a clear beginning, middle and end. The plot or key points should flow logically, and the paragraphs should clearly separate your ideas. Taking some time to plan your piece before you start writing will help you to achieve a strong, coherent structure.

You should develop an effective voice that is appropriate for the text type, purpose and audience and that allows you to explore ideas effectively. **Your grammar, spelling and punctuation must be correct**, unless you are purposefully bending the rules (e.g. to contribute to characterisation in dialogue).

**Write with fluency** and expression. Take time to read over your work and replace any clichéd or dull words or phrases with more precise and interesting ones. Check that you have varied your sentence structures and that your writing flows well.

Think about your target audience as you do this. Do your language choices suit their needs and help you to achieve your purpose?

There is greater scope for language choices and sentence structures in Section B than in Sections A and C. Depending on the type of text you write, you may consider using colloquial language and being more experimental with both structure and language.

### Mentor texts

Unlike the SAC task, the exam task does not require you to demonstrate that you are using a mentor text as a guide for effective writing or to base your ideas on those in the mentor texts. However, you do need to write an effective, well-structured piece, and the mentor texts you have studied will provide strong examples of this, so you may choose to draw on some of their writing strategies and approaches.

Remember that you should not produce more than one piece of writing for Section B, nor should you write a poem or song lyrics for this section.

# Section C: Analysis of argument and language

For this section of the exam, you have to write an analysis that shows your understanding of how the writer of a persuasive text uses argument and written and visual language to attempt to persuade their target audience to agree with their point of view on an issue. Your analysis needs to include discussion of the visual material included in the text.

## Assessment criteria

Your analysis will be assessed according to the criteria reproduced in the left-hand column in the following table. The right-hand column presents advice on how to address this criteria.

| Criteria | What you need to do |
|---|---|
| Understanding of contention, argument(s), and point of view | Clearly identify the writer's contention and main supporting reasons. |
| | Demonstrate an awareness of how the writer develops their argument (e.g. by presenting their reasons in a particular order). |

 

| Criteria | What you need to do |
|---|---|
| Analysis of the ways in which written and spoken language and visuals are used to present an argument(s) and to persuade an intended audience | Be specific about the target audience/s and consider how the writer has tried to cater for their prior knowledge, preferences, biases and characteristics. |
| | Refer to the text type (e.g. speech, opinion piece, newsletter) and identify how the writer has used features of this type persuasively. |
| | Use appropriate metalanguage to analyse the visual material, linking it to the argument and persuasive strategies in the written text. |
| Use of evidence from the text to support the analysis | Include relevant short quotations from the text in every paragraph to support your discussion. |
| | Link these examples to the persuasive strategies used by the writer: what is the intended impact on the reader? |
| | Comment on the overall persuasive approach of the writer and how persuasive strategies have a cumulative effect. |
| Use of fluent expression through appropriate use of vocabulary and conventions of Standard Australian English | Use appropriate metalanguage for analysing persuasive texts to help you communicate precisely and accurately. |
| | Vary the lengths of your sentences. |
| | Take time to read over your work and correct any grammar, spelling or punctuation errors. |

In addition to the assessment criteria listed above and on the previous page, your work will be assessed using the 'Expected qualities for the mark range – Section C', which can be found on the VCAA website: https://www.vcaa.vic.edu.au/assessment/vce/examination-specifications-past-examinations-and-examination-reports/english

The qualities necessary for essays to be scored in the top three mark ranges are reproduced on the next page. The distinguishing qualities of a Section C analysis worth nine to ten marks are highlighted.

| Marks | Expected qualities |
|---|---|
| 9–10 | Demonstrates a perceptive understanding of contention, the development of argument(s) as constructed in the text and the point of view expressed |
| | Demonstrates sophisticated insight into the ways in which written and spoken language and visuals complement the argument(s) and are used to persuade the intended audience |
| | Uses sophisticated and precise language |
| 8 | Demonstrates a thoughtful understanding of contention, the development of argument(s) as constructed in the text and the point of view expressed |
| | Demonstrates sound insight into the ways in which the written and spoken language and visuals work together to build the argument(s) and persuade the intended audience |
| | Uses language confidently |
| 7 | Demonstrates detailed understanding of contention, argument(s) presented in the text and the point of view expressed |
| | Demonstrates insight into the ways in which the written and spoken language and visuals in the text are used to persuade the intended audience |
| | Uses fluent expression |

## Features of high-, medium- and low-range responses

Previous exam reports have noted the following features of *high-range analyses*.

- They demonstrate understanding of the text's main purpose and summarise the writer's contention concisely and accurately.
- They identify the main target audience and link this explicitly to the writer's choices.
- They include analysis of both the argument and the language used to present it.
- They explore the implications of specific words or phrases, considering their connotations and their intended impact on the target audience.
- They analyse the visual material, referring to specific visual features and linking the point of view expressed to the written argument.
- They use precise and varied vocabulary and sentence structures to discuss the writer's choices and their intended impact on the audience.

 

Previous exam reports have noted the following features of *medium- to low-range analyses*.

- They summarise the text rather than analysing it.
- They fail to accurately identify the writer's main tone and why they might have employed this tone.
- They present generalised descriptions of persuasive techniques rather than showing an understanding of how a particular technique, word or phrase is used in a specific context to persuade the target audience.
- They neglect to analyse the visual material, simply describing it, or they fail to link its intended effects to those of the written text.
- They make little, if any, reference to the context, author, purpose or audience.
- They focus on analysing either just the argument or just the language, rather than presenting an integrated analysis of both.
- They attempt to evaluate the effectiveness of the writer's argument and language.

## Preparing for Section C

Use the following strategies to help you prepare for writing an analysis of argument and language.

**Read a wide variety of persuasive texts.** Make sure you are familiar with a range of persuasive text types and approaches to persuasion, so that you are prepared for whatever text type you see in the exam. Different structures and language choices are associated with different types of texts. Try to find written pieces that include one or two images and consider how the written and visual languages work together to persuade the target audience.

**Practise analysing the main persuasive elements of a text.** In the exam, you will need to read the task material and identify key elements quickly, so you can spend most of your time writing.

For each persuasive text you find, give yourself ten minutes to read the text and identify:

- the contention
- two or three supporting reasons
- how the writer sequences and builds on their argument, and the reasons for this
- the writer's purpose
- the main tone and any changes in tone, and the intended effect of these on the target audience

- three examples of persuasive language and their intended effects
- how the visual material works with the written text to present a point of view.

**Practise analysing the structure of persuasive texts.** Annotate each persuasive text you read to identify:

- how the writer begins
- the order of the supporting reasons or arguments
- where the writer argues against opposing points of view
- how the writer ends.

Make notes about the likely effect on the reader of putting the elements of the argument in this sequence. Why did the writer present them in this order?

**Practise analysing some persuasive examples.** Work with a partner to collect a range of sentences and phrases on a variety of issues. To drill down and analyse specific language choices, practise writing two or three analytical sentences about each of your examples. Consider the associations and connotations of particular words and pinpoint their intended emotional impact on the reader.

**Practise analysing visual language.** The visual component of the persuasive text is an important aspect that you are expected to analyse. Practise with visual texts such as cartoons, photographs, infographics and charts to identify features of visual texts and how they are used to persuade the viewer.

Revise metalanguage associated with visual texts and remember to consider how visual elements work together with written text to create a combined or overall persuasive effect. Think also about any text associated with the image, such as a caption, as well as the image's placement in the text. Does it connect to a particular section or aspect of the written text?

## Completing Section C

The following advice will help you to analyse how the writer's argumentative strategies and persuasive language support their attempt to persuade the chosen audience.

### Background information

This short paragraph tells you where the text was published or presented and some context surrounding the issue. It might also identify the intended audience. You should take these details into account in your analysis, to show that you understand how the writer has shaped the text for their audience and context; for example, by targeting certain emotions or appealing to possible audience biases.

 

The target audience could include one person, a few people or a large group of people. It will rarely be as broad as 'the general public'. Remember that a text might have more than one target audience, so pay attention to how the writer targets different groups; for example, a school newsletter might address both parents and students, and an open letter might address politicians as well as the voting public.

## Understanding the text

Read the passage carefully during the reading time and at least once more before attempting the task to ensure you understand the material. To successfully complete this task, you need to identify the:

- issue and context
- writer's name and position/affiliations (if relevant)
- text type
- place of publication/presentation
- audience
- writer's purpose.

Where possible, be specific when referring to the writer and the audience (e.g. the creator of the text might be a speaker, a parent, a spokesperson or a television presenter, while the audience might be readers of a particular newspaper, listeners of a podcast or attendees at a convention).

The table below summarises these key details from a Section C scenario in a VCAA sample exam.

| Key details | Examples |
|---|---|
| **Issue and context** | Feeding birds; writer is concerned about people feeding birds at a local park despite a sign advising them not to do so |
| **Writer's name and position** | Daphne Lower, member of the community |
| **Text type** | Post on a website |
| **Place of publication/ presentation** | *Strapleton Community Voice* website |
| **Audience** | Residents of the Strapleton area |
| **Purpose** | To encourage residents not to feed birds |

To do this task well, you must identify the intended audience. Often, this information is stated specifically in the background information. However, sometimes you need to infer who the audience is by reading the text carefully.

Remember, the audience will usually be more specific than just 'the general public'. Even if the text is, for example, an article in a daily newspaper, the author is usually focused primarily on a certain section of society (such as parents, car owners or residents of a particular area).

Some candidates performed poorly in a persuasive language task in an exam some years ago because they presumed that the audience was the general public, when the text (a letter) made it quite clear that the audience was one person – in this instance, the principal of a school.

You should also be able to identify the writer's contention. Express this in your introduction and be specific. For example, rather than saying 'The writer argues against dogs in parks', you should pinpoint the exact argument being presented: that dogs should be excluded from Beauty Park between the hours of 9 am and 6 pm.

## Annotating the text

Once you understand the text well and have identified its key aspects, your next step is to annotate it. Aim to clearly identify the writer's three or four main points of argument. You might like to underline the relevant parts of the text and make notes about the points of argument in dot-point form. You should also note how the argument is sequenced and structured.

Highlight examples of argument and persuasive language strategies. In the margins of the text, write annotations identifying these and the intended effects on the target audience.

Carefully choose which persuasive language examples you are going to analyse. You won't have time to analyse every example of persuasive language in a text. Focus on:

- examples of language use that you feel confident analysing
- persuasive techniques that are repeated in the text
- persuasive language that is especially powerful or noticeable.

You should also annotate the visual material, linking it clearly to one of the points or arguments you are analysing. Identify specific features of the visual material, using appropriate metalanguage where possible, and the intended effects on the audience.

Remember that your annotations will not be assessed.

Finally, create a brief plan by organising your annotations into points of argument. Number your notes according to the body paragraph in which you will discuss them.

## Considering structure

Writers make careful choices about how to present their overall argument. For example, they may save their most important reason until last to leave a powerful final impression. Or they may begin in a friendly tone or with a personal anecdote to get the audience onside, before shifting to a more aggressive tone or to hard-hitting facts and figures once they feel the audience is engaged.

In your analysis, refer to the overall shape of the argument and why it has been shaped in this way, to show that you have considered its structure as well as its content.

Remember that the sequencing of ideas and the placement and content of the image are all part of the writer's persuasive strategy.

## A holistic analysis

Analyse how argument, language and visuals *work together*. Do not treat these as separate elements of the text, since an audience's response will be influenced by all of them. Look at how language is used to present an argument and how an image reinforces reasons or pieces of evidence, all with the aim of achieving the writer's purpose.

Using strong, carefully chosen verbs will enable you to describe exactly what the writer is doing, how they are doing it and, most importantly, *why* they are doing it. Avoid repeating verbs such as 'positions' and 'persuades', which don't help you to give precise explanations. Verbs such as 'reinforces', 'emphasises', 'instils', 'elicits' and 'undermines' will help you to show a strong understanding of the language and the writer's intentions.

In your conclusion, you should summarise the writer's overall persuasive approach, commenting on how argument and language techniques work together to target specific emotions and responses in the audience.

ANALYSE

**Work in a small group of four or five people for this activity.**

1. **Individually, find a persuasive text with accompanying visual material.**
2. **In your group, share your texts. Make notes on the purpose, target audience, contention, tone and supporting reasons in each text.**
3. **Highlight four or five examples of persuasive strategies used in each text and make notes about their intended effects on the reader.**
4. **Make notes on the persuasive effect of the visual language. Focus on two or three elements of the visual material and identify their intended effects on the viewer.**
5. **Compare your answers. Discuss any similarities and differences in your responses.**

## Proofreading and revising

Try to finish writing all your responses in the exam with five to ten minutes to spare. This gives you time to read your answers and identify errors or ways to improve your work. The list below identifies what you should look for.

- In Section A, your text response clearly addresses the topic.
- In Section B, you have effectively incorporated the title and at least one piece of stimulus material into your text, your target audience and intended purpose are clear, and your writing explicitly connects to your Framework.
- In Section C, you have analysed both the big-picture elements of the persuasive text (e.g. the writer's purpose, contention and reasons) and some of the finer detail (e.g. particularly persuasive words and phrases).
- Each piece is of a reasonable length and is finished, with a clear conclusion or ending.
- Each piece flows well (add some linking words or revise your paragraphing if needed).
- No words have been omitted or incorrectly repeated.
- Spelling, punctuation and grammar are correct.
- Quotations are enclosed in quotation marks.
- There is no uninteresting or imprecise vocabulary (replace any that you find with stronger word choices).
- All words are legible (neatly cross out and rewrite any that are not).